Everton
in the 1980s

Everton
in the 1980s

Phil Thompson & Steve Hale

TEMPUS

This book is dedicated to Frank, a great friend of Steve Hale, and Phil Jackson. Both are true Blues.

Frontispiece: Goodison Park

First published 2003

Tempus Publishing Limited
The Mill, Brimscombe Port,
Stroud, Gloucestershire, GL5 2QG

British Library Cataloguing in Publication Data.
A catalogue record for this book is available from the British Library.

ISBN 0 7524 2952 3

Typesetting and origination by Tempus Publishing Limited
Printed in Great Britain by Midway Colour Print, Wiltshire

Contents

Introduction   7

one   The Midfield General Arrives   11

two   The Iceman Cometh:
The Signing of Andy Gray, 1983   23

three   The Great Escape at Oxford, 1984   31

four   Blues and Reds Together:
The Milk Cup Final, 1984   35

five   The FA Cup Comes Back
to Goodison, 1984   41

six   The League Championship and
That Graeme Sharp Goal, 1985   51

seven   From Dublin to Rotterdam:
The European Cup Winners' Cup, 1985   69

eight   The Double Fantasy, 1985   85

nine   So Near and Yet So Far, 1986   97

ten   The Clash of the Titans: The First
All-Merseyside FA Cup Final, 1986   107

eleven   Howard Kendall's Swansong:
Champions Again, 1987   115

Bibliography   127

Howard Kendall became the new Everton manager in May 1981. It took time, but he was destined to become the greatest Everton FC manager in the club's famous history.

Introduction

'When I went to watch games at Goodison during my period as Blackburn Manager, Evertonians would constantly ask me: 'When are you coming back to Everton, Howard?'

Howard Kendall

The names of Howard Kendall and Everton Football Club will always be intrinsically linked. Quite simply, Howard Kendall is without any doubt the greatest Everton FC manager of all time. Many Evertonians will bestow this accolade on the man who took them to two League titles and FA Cup success in the 1960s, Harry Catterick. But it was Kendall who equalled Catterick's domestic triumphs, as well as bringing the one thing that Evertonians have never enjoyed before or since, the capture of a major European trophy. For one brief season the blue half of Merseyside could lord it over their Anfield rivals for whom success in Europe was almost second nature.

When Everton won the European Cup Winners' Cup in 1985, it was not just the fact that they had at long last won a European trophy but the style in which they had achieved this success that made the whole of the European football fraternity sit up and take notice. Kendall's team were widely acknowledged as one of the most talented outfits in Europe and were strongly fancied to take the European Cup the following season. Whether they would or wouldn't have achieved success in Europe's greatest club competition is, after the tragic Heysel Stadium disaster in May 1985, something the players and fans will never know.

Neither Liverpool Football Club nor the majority of their supporters were responsible for the Heysel tragedy. But the aftermath would hit English clubs, and Everton in particular, severely. The facts are that a few hours before the Liverpool-Juventus European Cup final was due to begin, a contingent of Liverpool 'supporters' charged at a group of Juventus fans, driving them into the corner of a stadium that was patently not of the required standard to hold such a prestigious final. A wall collapsed and many

Italians were trampled during the panic and confusion. The final death toll of thirty-nine Juventus supporters, along with many injuries, led to the implementation of a ban on English clubs playing in all European competitions. Football is not more important than life and death, but the majority of Everton fans and players from the 1980s era firmly believe that the European ban denied the club of probable success in the European Cup in 1986 and also in 1988.

Dreams of conquering Europe were, however, the furthest thing from Howard Kendall's mind when he was welcomed back into the Goodison fold in the summer of 1981. Everton under Gordon Lee had just finished fifteenth in the League and were going nowhere. When Lee had first arrived at the club, initial signs had been encouraging. He had accepted the Everton job with them positioned near the foot of the table, and results and the level of performance did improve. There was also the added bonus of Everton reaching a Wembley final for the first time since the halcyon days of Harry Catterick and the 1968 Everton-West Brom FA Cup final. Everton eventually went on to lose the 1977 League Cup final after two hard-fought replays against Aston Villa, but Gordon Lee during his first few seasons at Goodison certainly revived the club's fortunes. The improvement, however, was not maintained and at the end of a dreadful 1980/81 season disillusioned Evertonians were granted their wish and Gordon Lee was dismissed. The announcement by the Everton board that one of Goodison's favourite sons was to become the new manager was met with firm approval by the Everton faithful. Kendall was, after all, firmly established in Goodison history as one of the greatest players ever to represent the club, and as a member of the midfield trio of Alan Ball, Colin Harvey and Howard Kendall in the sensational 1970 championship-winning side, he was one of that threesome affectionately dubbed in later years as 'The Holy Trinity' by the Everton fans.

After learning the managerial ropes, first as a player-coach under Alan Durban at Stoke, then as player-manager at Blackburn, Kendall was keen to test his ability in the top flight. Kendall had almost led Blackburn to promotion to the First Division in his final season with them and was due to accompany his players on an end of season holiday to Spain. When news broke of Gordon Lee's departure from Everton, the Blackburn players knew that their talented young boss would probably not be with them for the start of the new season. Derek Fazackerley, a Blackburn player at the time, recalled:

'At the end of the season we were all going to Spain and it was the worst kept secret that Howard was leaving us to join Everton. We had to report to Ewood Park on a Sunday morning. Howard walked over to the lads on the coach and said: "Sorry I can't be with you. Thanks for everything. Hope to see you all in the First Division soon." I don't think he was an emotional sort of fellow. To be fair in management I don't think you can afford to be. As the coach pulled away Howard was standing by himself. But he was probably thinking: "Right, it's Everton now."'

Howard Kendall was under no illusions about the task that lay ahead of him at Everton. But amongst the primarily journeymen professionals that Kendall inherited were two young players that Gordon Lee had brought to the club. They would become an integral part of what would become the great Everton team of the mid-eighties: Kevin Ratcliffe and Graeme Sharp. Sharp had been signed by Gordon Lee from Dumbarton for £120,000 in April 1980. Aberdeen's bright young manager, Alex Ferguson, had been keen to take Sharp to Aberdeen, but it was Lee and Everton who won the chase. At first, Sharp was unsettled at Goodison and an incident during his debut, away to Brighton, did little to improve his opinion of life in the English First Division. He recalls:

> 'I made my debut for the first team at Brighton. I'd only been on the field for ten minutes and my first introduction to the English game was to get a right hook off their centre half. I don't think I got a kick, just a punch. So it made me stand back and think, have I done the right thing leaving Scotland?'

Plagued by lack of belief in his ability and homesickness, Graeme Sharp struggled during his first seasons at Everton. Everton reserve team coach, Colin Harvey, another member of the great midfield trio of the late 1960s, worked hard on injecting confidence into Sharp's game but it would not be until the arrival of a fellow Scot, the battle-hardened warrior Andy Gray in 1983, that the young striker would blossom into one of the greatest centre forwards Everton fans had ever seen.

Kevin Ratcliffe had joined Everton as a youth and he made his debut against Manchester United at Old Trafford in 1980. Under Gordon Lee and then during the early period of Kendall's managership, Ratcliffe struggled to establish himself in the first team, and when he did play he considered himself to be playing out of position at left-back. Eventually, like Graeme Sharp, Kevin Ratcliffe was to mature into an outstanding performer for the club, but at one stage it was touch and go that he would even stay at Goodison Park.

Apart from Ratcliffe and Sharp, Howard Kendall also inherited two other Everton youngsters who would go on to become special talents; Gary Stevens and Steve McMahon. Sadly, McMahon, who made his Goodison debut during the Lee regime, was to become the one that got away when Kendall reluctantly sold him to Aston Villa in 1983. Gary Stevens, a future England star at full-back, was given his Everton debut by Kendall in 1981. When you consider that also on Everton's books when Kendall arrived was Mark Higgins, who looked to be a certain England centre half in the future, and the highly talented tough Liverpool-born full-back John Bailey, Everton's new boss was hardly joining a club that was bereft of talent. All that was needed was a man to build on the undoubted potential that already existed at Goodison, hopefully supplemented by some new arrivals. It would take time, but eventually Howard Kendall would prove himself to be that man. The man would give the blue half of Merseyside the success they had craved for years.

Mark Higgins in action against Manchester United. Higgins looked to have an outstanding future ahead of him when Kendall arrived at Everton in 1981. International honours were predicted for the commanding central defender, before injury cruelly brought his Everton career to an end at just twenty-five years of age.

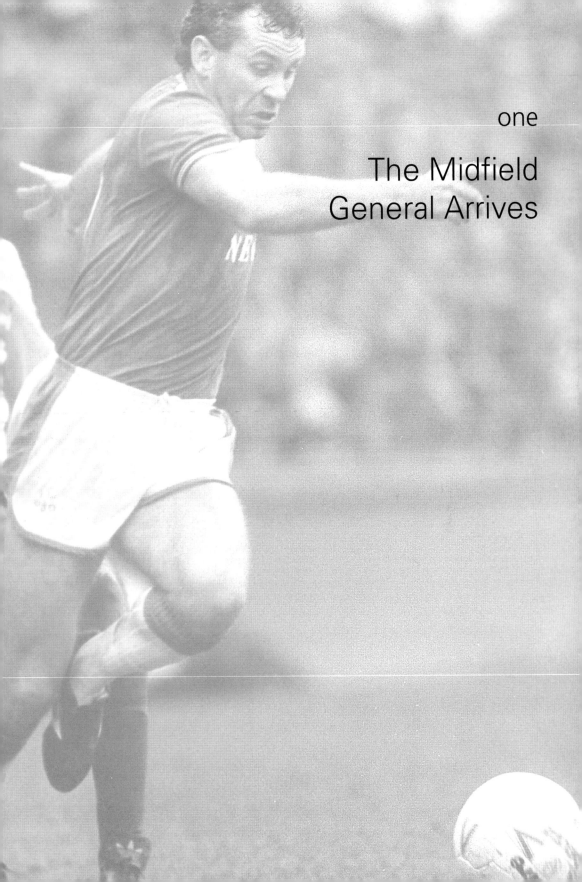

one

The Midfield
General Arrives

Peter Reid in action against Aston Villa. Howard Kendall described Reid as: 'Everton's most important signing since the Second World War.'

'In December 1982 I made what was to prove, I think, Everton's most important signing since the Second World War – Peter Reid from Bolton for £60,000.'

Howard Kendall

At the start of Howard Kendall's first season in charge, Everton fans saw the introduction of a whole host of new faces. Jim Arnold was now in goal, but the keeper who was destined to become a future Goodison great, Neville Southall, was significantly now also in the squad. Alan Ainscow began the season in midfield along with Welsh international Mickey Thomas, recently acquired from Manchester United. Up front, Alan Biley and Mick Ferguson vied for the striker's role alongside Peter Eastoe. Anticipation was high and after a 3-1 victory over Birmingham in the opening game, Evertonians looked forward to the rest of the season with renewed confidence. It was to be another three weeks, however, before Everton would taste victory again.

By Christmas, Everton had lost two of their midfield stars. Asa Hartford left to join Manchester City and Mickey Thomas, after refusing to play for the reserves, joined Brighton. Thomas had made just eleven appearances for the club. Everton finished the season in eighth position, a solid improvement on Gordon Lee's last season at the club but still not nearly enough to satisfy the Goodison faithful who had to put up with their Anfield rivals winning the League Championship yet again.

Another crucial signing made during the course of Kendall's first season in charge, Adrian Heath for £700,000 from Stoke, would prove to be highly significant in years to come. Howard Kendall, although obviously hoping for much better, was quietly satisfied with his opening campaign. He said:

'When I first arrived at the club I made changes. Some of them turned out to be disasters and some turned out to be very successful. Maybe I should have taken more time, but I felt I had to make an immediate impact. Eighth place was certainly more comfortable than the struggles against relegation. In fact, we only missed qualifying for Europe by one place.'

And speaking about Everton's record signing of Adrian Heath, Kendall had no doubts that he would become a success: 'Adrian took a little time to settle but he is a great player, a tremendous worker. You don't have to motivate him. He's got a hell of an engine on him.'

Above: *The Everton squad at the beginning of the 1982/83 season. From left to right, back row: Ratcliffe, Wright, Walsh, Southall, Arnold, Higgins, Ferguson, Mountfield. Middle row: Harvey, Johnson, Irvine, Richardson, Sharp, Borrows, King, Stevens, Heaton, Clinkard. Front row: Sheedy, McMahon, Heath, Kendall, Ross, Bailey, Ainscow.*

Left: *Jim Arnold, who joined Everton from Blackburn Rovers in August 1981. Arnold lost his place in the Everton goal to future Goodison great Neville Southall in 1983. He continued as a valuable squad member until joining Port Vale in 1985.*

Opposite: *The Everton chairman at the time of Howard Kendall's arrival at Goodison Park in 1981, Sir Philip Carter. Without Carter's brave backing of Kendall when the majority of Evertonians were desperate to see the Everton boss sacked at the end of 1983, it is highly probable that the golden period of the mid-1980s would never have happened.*

The start of the new season saw the breaking of an unwritten rule between the two Liverpool clubs that had lasted for nearly twenty years. When Everton signed Kevin Sheedy from Liverpool for £100,000, it was the first transfer dealing between the Merseyside giants since Liverpool reluctantly sold their tough little winger, Johnny Morrissey, to Everton in 1962. If Morrissey was a steal at £10,000, Sheedy was the bargain of the century, even at ten times that amount twenty years later. When Everton decided to give another Liverpool reject, Alan Harper, a chance at Goodison in 1983 – with mightily impressive results – it was no wonder that the Anfield club were beginning to get a complex about allowing their players to join their city rivals when they left Anfield.

Liverpool did, however, get their own back a few years later when Steve McMahon ended up giving them great service after Aston Villa sold him to the Reds. Kevin Sheedy, talking about his transfer from Liverpool to Everton in a newspaper article at the time, recalled with more than a hint of bitterness:

'You may have noticed that not many players that are on the fringe of the first team at Liverpool leave them and build a successful career with another big club. I found out why – Liverpool like to choose a club for you. They told me they'd had offers for me but wouldn't identify the clubs, which made me think that

Left: *Colin Harvey, idolised as a player at Everton in the 1960s and early 1970s. Harvey was promoted to first team coach in 1984. Along with fellow first team coach Mick Heaton and manager Howard Kendall, they produced an outstanding Everton team in the mid-1980s.*

Opposite: *Neville Southall, probably the greatest goalkeeper in Everton's history and an invaluable member of the great 1980s side at Goodison.*

some were from big clubs. I could have stayed at Liverpool and had the occasional first team game but I wasn't prepared to waste away like that. I wanted to make my own decisions, which I did when my contract ran out. I think signing for Everton upset Liverpool because I think they realised that I could do well at Goodison Park.'

Liverpool's loss was Everton's gain and Kevin Sheedy became one of the greatest left-sided midfielders in the history of the club. Another Kendall bargain buy was the Tranmere Rovers defender Derek Mountfield. Mountfield made the short journey across the River Mersey for just £30,000 and, like Sheedy, would become an integral member of the great Everton team of the mid-eighties. Mountfield made his Everton debut away to Birmingham but would have to wait until the following season before he became a first team regular. Everton opened the new season in some style with home victories against Aston Villa and Spurs, knocking in eight goals in the process. It was to prove a

false dawn, however, and a disastrous 5-0 home defeat against Liverpool confirmed to Evertonians that the return of the good times to Goodison were still a distant dream.

In goal for Everton that bleak November day was Neville Southall. Southall's international team-mate Ian Rush had a field day against the Blues knocking in an incredible four goals. Recalling Liverpool's rout of Everton in his autobiography, Rush said:

> 'In the 1982/83 season I had some memorable moments. We won the League Championship and the League Cup, but the highlight had to be scoring four against Everton. Neville Southall was my old pal from the Welsh team. Poor Neville was so shell-shocked after that game he was left out of the Everton team until near the end of the season.'

Southall went on loan to Port Vale but returned, confidence restored, to the Everton team for the final games of the season. Howard Kendall knew there was something

special about Neville Southall, and the Everton manager's faith in the Welsh keeper would be richly rewarded in sensational style during future campaigns. Remembering Southall's early days at the club, Kevin Ratcliffe was struck by how overwhelmed the young goalkeeper appeared to be by signing for a big club:

'These days Neville is known for speaking his mind, but when he first arrived at the club from Bury he was very shy. No disrespect to Bury but I reckon our training ground was bigger than Gigg Lane! But being alongside outgoing people like Peter Reid and Andy Gray probably brought Neville out of his shell, and now you can't stop him.'

The signing of Peter Reid in December of 1982 has been acknowledged by Howard Kendall as one of the most important pieces of transfer business in Everton's history. For just £60,000 the club had obtained a player who became a major influence on Everton Football Club, both on the field of play and in the dressing room. Initially, the injury

Above: *Terry Curran, who was a popular Kendall loan signing from Sheffield United at the end of 1983. Curran returned to Sheffield but eventually signed for Everton at the beginning of the 1983/84 season. The gifted winger failed to establish a regular first team spot and left on a free transfer in 1985.*

Opposite: *Neville Southall.*

Above: *The tenacious Peter Reid comes away with the ball after another full-blooded midfield encounter.*

Opposite: *Alan Harper seen here in action against his old club in a 1986 derby game. Harper joined the Blues in 1983 after failing to make the first team breakthrough at Anfield. Able to play in a variety of positions, Harper's finest moment in his Everton career was probably his FA Cup semi-final opening goal against Sheffield Wednesday in 1986.*

jinx that had blighted his career at Bolton looked to have accompanied him to Goodison Park as well. Reid had already sustained two broken legs and a host of other injuries during his Burden Park days, and after just seven games for Everton was on the injury list again. Reid did not regain full fitness until the following season but when he did Evertonians were unanimous in their verdict that Peter Reid was the most combative midfielder that they had seen at the club since the days of the great Alan Ball in the 1960s.

Despite the loss of Reid after just a handful of games, Everton did finish the season with something of a flourish, losing only six of their final twenty-one games. Neville Southall was also now back in goal, and the rapidly maturing Kevin Ratcliffe was playing in his favoured position at centre-back. With the summer signing of Trevor Steven for £300,000 compensating for the disappointing loss of Steve McMahon to Aston Villa, prospects for the new season looked promising.

Graeme Sharp celebrates after scoring yet another goal for Everton. Sharp holds the record as Everton's top post-war goalscorer. An integral member of the great 1980s side, Sharp was once selected by Ian Rush as the one striker in the world that he would like to play alongside given the opportunity.

Liverpool's Craig Johnston feels the force of Everton's Kevin Ratcliffe during a Merseyside derby encounter in 1984. Ratcliffe captained Everton during their golden trophy-winning period of the 1980s.

two

The Iceman Cometh:
The Signing of
Andy Gray, 1983

Andy Gray in action on his Everton home debut against Nottingham Forest, 1983.

24

'Andy Gray never used to train. "The Ice Man", we called him, because he always had ice on his knees. I don't know how he passed a medical, but he was our leader, with Reidy.'

John Bailey

If Everton had finished their previous season with renewed optimism, within weeks of the new campaign the Goodison Park regulars were growing more restless with each passing day. By mid-September, Everton were near the foot of the First Division table. Only six of the first twenty-one games resulted in victories. Liverpool had beaten their city rivals with embarrassing ease 3-0 in a live televised game. Attendance figures at Goodison Park were on a downward spiral and the future, for Howard Kendall, looked bleak. Only 8,000 turned up for a midweek Milk Cup match against Chesterfield. One ray of light amid the Goodison gloom was the signing of battle-hardened warrior Andy Gray.

Kendall was desperate to find a player who could put the ball into the net. Like Peter Reid, Gray was injury-ridden but when fit the big Scot was just the type of player that Kendall had been scouring the country looking for, and at £200,000 he looked a bargain. Gray's contract with Wolves was due to expire and with the Molineux club looking a certainty to be relegated at the end of the season, playing in the Second Division was not a prospect that appealed to the Scottish international. With the expiry of Gray's contract in mind, Wolves were keen to obtain a fee for him while they could. The deal suited all parties. Everton had acquired an experienced international centre forward for a relatively small fee.

If the signing of Andy Gray would prove crucial in the revival of Everton, the promotion of Howard Kendall's 'Holy Trinity' team-mate, Colin Harvey, from reserve-team to first-team coach would also be highly significant in the long term. Everton captain Kevin Ratcliffe had no doubts that Harvey's promotion was a major factor in the upturn in Everton Football Club's fortune. In his autobiography he stated:

'There will be people pointing to Andy Gray and Peter Reid. Both were terrific in what they did. But Colin was the man. There's no doubt in my mind about who was the key man in Everton's revival. I've never met anyone like him. He's one of that rare breed who will get another ten per cent out of you, even if you haven't got it to give. He snarls at you, winds you up. But he has tremendous respect from the lads because he'd done it as a player.'

Andy Gray, the gladiatorial Scot who set Goodison alight after being signed from Wolves at the end of 1983. Evertonians had not witnessed such brave displays of centre forward play since the days of Dave Hickson in the 1950s. Gray, along with Peter Reid, was Everton's leader in the dressing-room and spearheaded the club's trophy-winning campaigns of the mid-1980s. It is hard to believe that he was at the club for less than two years, such was the galvanising effect he had on everyone at Goodison Park.

Initially, the signing of Andy Gray and Colin Harvey's first-team coaching appointment failed to make any impact at all. A woeful 0-0 Christmas period draw at home to Sunderland, followed a few days later by a humiliating 3-0 defeat at Wolves, saw the morale of Everton's players and supporters at an all-time low. Howard Kendall was under intense pressure and his old friend from his Stoke days, Alan Durban, witnessed the Boxing Day debacle against Sunderland: 'I was at Goodison on Boxing Day 1983 and Everton had their lowest gate of the season. The crowd were chanting, "Kendall out! Kendall out!"' Andy Gray, recalling Everton's disastrous Christmas, said: 'The pressure was beginning to build. The "Kendall Out" campaign was stronger than ever, and if not for the admirable support of Everton chairman Philip Carter the club would have been looking for a new manager. Many clubs would have sacked Howard Kendall there and then.' Howard Kendall, recalling his darkest hour at Goodison, said: 'There were demands that I should either resign or be sacked. Leaflets asking for my head were circulated. They said: "Thirty thousand stay-at-home fans can't be wrong. Bring back attractive football to Goodison Park. Howard Kendall and Philip Carter out."'

Philip Carter's reluctance to sack his manager was to prove brave and ultimately, as it turned out, one of the most fortunate decisions in Everton's history. Everton star of the

Graeme Sharp narrowly fails to convert a scoring opportunity. Sharp's Everton career hit the heights after Andy Gray arrived at the club. Kevin Ratcliffe once said: 'Andy taught Sharpy a few tricks of the trade. Graeme grew meaner. His touch and confidence improved until he was 100% better.'

1960s, Derek Temple, told *The Liverpool Echo*: 'Philip Carter must get a lot of credit for sticking by Howard Kendall when the going got tough. When the pressure is on many clubs relieve it by sacking the manager. At one point it did look like Howard was going to get the push.' There can be little doubt that if Howard Kendall had bowed to what the majority of the Evertonians were crying out for and departed the Goodison Park stage, the glory days of the mid-eighties would have never happened and we would probably still be harking back to the 1960s as Everton's only post-war golden period.

But Philip Carter in a newspaper interview was adamant that the Everton board had never at any stage considered relieving Kendall of his duties:

'If things had continued to go from bad to worse, we should have had to admit that we had made a mistake, but it never came close to that. We realised that we were going to have a period of rebuilding and consolidation. We knew what Howard was trying to do. We knew when we appointed him that he had limited experience but bags of potential.'

Above: *Kevin Ratcliffe and Graeme Souness toss up before the March 1984 Goodison derby game. Harper and Rush scored in a 1-1 draw.*

Opposite: *Andy Gray celebrates another goal at Goodison.*

The Everton board's decision to back their manager was to pay off in dramatic style as the 1983/84 season unfolded. The beginning of the New Year found Everton playing away to his old club Birmingham, and before the game Kendall read the riot act to his beleaguered team. Pulling no punches he told them straight that if results did not improve then their days in the Everton first-team were numbered. The Everton boss's ultimatum did the trick and goals from King and Stevens gave them a comfortable victory. A few days later Everton played Stoke in the FA Cup and Howard Kendall employed an almost Shanklyesque-style psychological pep talk to gee-up his men before the game. Aware of the vast army of Evertonians travelling to the game and the noise they were making before kick-off, the Everton boss opened the dressing-room window and said: 'Listen to that support. You can't let those people down, can you? Go out there and do it for them.' Kendall's ploy worked and Everton eased through to the next round of the FA Cup with a 2-0 victory.

Over the years Evertonians have debated what was the defining moment of the team's and Howard Kendall's fortunes during the start of their 1980s golden period. Adrian Heath's equalising goal in the Milk Cup at Oxford is often put forward as the moment when the rise to glory began. But the 6 January 1984 FA Cup victory at Stoke City is the moment that Everton captain Kevin Ratcliffe claims was the beginning of the sun shining over Goodison Park again. 'That was the moment we took off,' claims Ratcliffe.

Andy Gray salutes the Evertonians after scoring.

three

The Great Escape at Oxford, 1984

Adrian Heath scores against Queen's Park Rangers in Everton's 3-1 victory, 1984.

'Howard Kendall said to me recently, "You scored nearly 100 goals for Everton and all you're remembered for is that goal at Oxford in the League Cup!"'

Adrian Heath

The early months of 1984 saw a dramatic change in Everton's fortunes. Before and during the Christmas 1983 period the team had looked like a bunch of strangers who were frightened to go out and display their undoubted talent. Suddenly, they were looking forward with relish to each League and cup game on the agenda. Howard Kendall was still at this stage under pressure. The sceptical, of whom there were many, believed that Everton's encouraging start to 1984 was probably just a flash-in-the-pan. And when Everton found themselves facing an ignominious exit to Oxford in the Milk Cup quarter-final on 18 January, the knives were out for Kendall again. Losing 1-0 with just ten minutes' play left, Oxford defender Kevin Brock made a poor back-pass to his goalkeeper. Adrian Heath pounced on the defender's mistake, rounded the keeper and slotted the ball into the net. Everton had scraped a draw but thrashed Oxford 4-1 in the replay.

Just how important was the goal by the player that the Evertonians dubbed 'Inchy' because of his diminutive size in the club's history? Adrian Heath himself believes that Andy Gray's goal at Stoke in the FA Cup tie a few weeks earlier was far more crucial. He said: 'The goal I scored at Oxford was not the most important one. I reckon it was Andy Gray's at Stoke. That was a game we had to win to try and begin to believe in ourselves. That game was the one that convinced us that we might have turned the corner.' To Howard Kendall, however, Heath's Oxford goal was a defining moment in the Everton manager's career: 'If ever I was looking at a team that wasn't going to score it was Everton at Oxford that night. I was fairly confident that our run in the Milk Cup was over. I'd have been sacked if we'd lost, or at least that's what people tell me.'

Everton's great escape at the Manor Ground was ultimately to lead to the first ever all-Merseyside Wembley final against their Anfield rivals. But the early rounds of the Milk Cup competition were to provide a mixture of dour, nail-biting and hard-fought encounters. Everton began the competition with a two-legged tie against Chesterfield. Graeme Sharp gave Everton a one-goal advantage for the return at Goodison two weeks later. Everton only managed to scrape a 2-2 draw in the home tie and were heckled and booed off the pitch after the final whistle. In the next round against Coventry at Goodison, two late goals from Heath and Sharp gave Everton another hard-fought 2-1 victory. Just over 8,000 attended the game, the majority of Evertonians showing little interest in witnessing how their club fared in the Milk Cup at this stage of the competition.

Everton were drawn away to West Ham in the next round, and a 2-2 draw brought them back to Goodison for a pre-Christmas replay. Goals from Andy King and Kevin Sheedy set up a quarter-final tie against Oxford. Oxford had already beaten Leeds, Newcastle and Manchester United on their way to the quarter-finals, so facing a beleaguered Everton team held few fears for them. After their fortunate 1-1 draw at the Manor Ground, goals from Heath, Sharp, Sheedy and Richardson set up a semi-final two-leg game against Aston Villa. They were just two games away from a Wembley final. It may have been the lesser of the three domestic competitions, but Everton were desperate to have a taste of the glory that their rivals Liverpool seemed to have obtained for season after season since the start of the 1970s. The stage was set for an Everton hero to emerge and midfielder Kevin Richardson's display in the first leg at Goodison was heroic in the extreme. Despite suffering a fractured and dislocated wrist in the early stages, he played through the pain-barrier for three-quarters of the game and even scored Everton's second goal in a 2-0 victory. Although Villa pushed them hard with a 1-0 victory in the second leg, Everton held out to reach the Milk Cup final. Their opponents would be their Merseyside rivals, Liverpool. Howard Kendall was overjoyed to have taken his team to Wembley. He told the press: 'At long last Everton have reached a Wembley final. The disappointing thing is that we shall be playing Liverpool on their own ground!'

One of the Everton heroes in their semi-final success over Aston Villa was Alan Irvine, now a key member of David Moyes' backroom staff at Goodison. Recalling the scenes of jubilation at Villa Park in February 1984, Irvine told *The Liverpool Echo*:

'On the final whistle I was over on the far side of the pitch, well away from the players' tunnel. I started to make my way over and was about ten yards from the entrance when I was swamped by fans. They carried me hand and foot across the pitch. It was a fabulous feeling, a memory I will never forget. They were absolutely brilliant!'

four

Blues and Reds Together:
The Milk Cup Final, 1984

A poignant moment after Everton's Maine Road Milk Cup defeat as Liverpool's Sammy Lee consoles a tearful Everton captain Kevin Ratcliffe.

'It was billed as the friendly final, but I'll tell you what, it was definitely not friendly on the pitch.'

Adrian Heath

Everton's 1984 revival that had seen them reach the Milk Cup final was also accompanied by a huge improvement in their League form and success in the early rounds of the FA Cup. Everton lost just three League games in the period from January to the end of the season in May. Suddenly everything clicked. From goalkeeper Neville Southall through to new signing Andy Gray, there was a confidence and a buzz about the team. Peter Reid had shaken off his injury problems and was developing into the outstanding midfield battler that Howard Kendall always knew he was capable of becoming. Most of all there was a battling quality about the whole team that would become the foundation on which much of their future success would be built. Nobody relished the prospect of facing Everton in the mid-eighties. Apart from being a team liberally sprinkled with highly-gifted players, they were also a tough outfit who had few fears when it came to facing the more physical teams in the First Division.

Andy Gray had been cup-tied for Everton's Milk Cup adventures, but in the League and FA Cup he more than proved his worth. He brought life and urgency to the dressing room. Gray didn't have a negative thought in his head and he demanded that his team-mates were the same. Everton captain Kevin Ratcliffe claimed that Gray's greatest legacy was the impact that he had on Graeme Sharp. Ratcliffe said: 'Aggression wasn't part of Graeme's game, but it was the key to Andy's. He taught Sharpy a few tricks of the trade. Graeme grew meaner. His touch and confidence improved until he was 100 per cent better.'

Apart from the impact Andy Gray was having on the team, there was also the Colin Harvey factor. Harvey commanded a huge amount of respect from the players. Full-back Gary Stevens, who had by now forced his way into the first-team, recalled his early impressions of Harvey:

'When I first joined the club as an apprentice, Colin was reserve-team coach. He made it his business to put newcomers to the test, both physically and mentally. He used to join in training sessions so that he could kick and foul you to try and provoke a reaction. It was his way of seeing what you were made of and he always preferred the 110 per cent man to the ball player.'

Harvey had built his reputation at Everton as a 110 per cent type of player during the Catterick era and it was clear to see that the Harvey work ethic was an integral part of Everton's newly-acquired determination and fighting spirit.

In the 1984 Milk Cup final, with Everton's growing confidence and determination well to the fore, Liverpool had to put all of their Wembley experience and undoubted ability to good use to contain the Blues. Before the game, the whole of British football could only sit back in wonderment and envy at the sight of supposedly bitter rivals standing side by side supporting their heroes. This was the way sport was supposed to be, but rarely was in modern-day football. Even today, the fondest memories of the players who participated in the historic first all-Merseyside Wembley final was the sight of blues and reds together when they entered the field of play. Recalling the occasion, Everton's John Bailey remarked: 'We were a Liverpool and Everton family – some supported one, some supported the other. Walking out of the tunnel, the noise, the cheering, the red and blue, no segregation. You wouldn't see that anywhere in the world. I'll take that memory to my grave.' Adrian Heath spoke in the same vein. He recalled, 'That is a day I'll never forget. It was a fantastic sight seeing the red and blue colours everywhere. It was billed as the friendly final, but I'll tell you what, it was definitely not friendly on the pitch. In all the derby games I've played, none was as passionate as that one.'

The game itself resulted in a 0-0 draw, though Evertonians to this day claim that they were denied a blatant penalty when Alan Hansen appeared to stop a goal-bound Adrian Heath on the line by scooping the ball away with his hand. The replay at Maine Road resulted in a Graeme Souness goal winning the Milk Cup for Liverpool. The Evertonians were devastated but their team had shown over the two finals that they now had a team at Goodison who were capable of competing with the best. Liverpool boss Joe Fagan acknowledged that his team had been pushed hard over the two games when he said after the game: 'A lot of Evertonians will go home crying tonight, but they needn't. They should be proud of their team.'

Above: *A dejected Alan Harper sits on the turf at Maine Road after a Graeme Souness goal defeated Everton in the Milk Cup final replay against Liverpool, 1984.*

Opposite: *Adrian Heath in action during the all-Merseyside Milk Cup final of 1984. The game finished in a 0-0 stalemate.*

The Everton team who returned to Wembley before the start of the 1984/85 season and gained revenge on Liverpool by defeating them in the Charity Shield 1-0. From left to right, back row: Richardson, Reid, Bailey, Steven, Ratcliffe, Southall. Front row: Heath, Mountfield, Sharp, Stevens, Bracewell.

five

The FA Cup Comes Back
to Goodison, 1984

Adrian Heath scores the winner against Southampton in the FA Cup semi-final of 1984. The game was played at Highbury.

'It was important to win the FA Cup. It would bring a trophy back to Goodison Park for the first time in fourteen years. It would reward our loyal fans and it would mean Everton were back in Europe.'

Howard Kendall

The importance of winning the FA Cup in 1984 cannot be overestimated. Everton had shown in the Milk Cup final against Liverpool that they were back, but they now needed a trophy to reinforce to the Goodison regulars that this was not another false dawn. The decline of Everton had certainly been reversed but something tangible to really celebrate was needed. Everton's path to the FA Cup semi-final was achieved after victories against Stoke, Gillingham, Shrewsbury and Notts County. Everton took three matches to dispose of Gillingham. After drawing the first game at Goodison, Gillingham took them back to a replay on their own ground and almost snatched the game in the final minutes. Tony Cascarino was put through on goal with only Southall to beat. The Everton keeper pulled off a fine save to take the tie to a third game. Two goals from Sheedy and one from Heath put them through and to Neville Southall this was the crucial moment in Everton's season: 'Everyone says that the Oxford game was the turning point. I thought Gillingham was the turning point for us. We played three games. We went down there, drew 0-0 and got absolutely battered. I think that was a good result.'

In the semi-final Everton met Southampton at Highbury. Everton had narrowly beaten Southampton 1-0 at Goodison through an Andy Gray goal two weeks before the semi-final, and another close encounter was anticipated. Southampton had the veteran striker Frank Worthington leading their attack and Everton were only too aware that he was still capable of winning any game with one piece of magic. Kevin Ratcliffe and Derek Mountfield kept Worthington under a tight rein but neither side managed to make the breakthrough in the first ninety minutes of play.

Ratcliffe knew that Worthington had no more to give in the extra-time period when he approached the Everton defender to shake hands at the end of the game. When Ratcliffe informed him that there was extra-time, Worthington's face dropped as he exclaimed: 'Oh no, it's not, is it?' A crucial extra-time winner from Adrian Heath took Everton to their first FA Cup final since they played West Brom at Wembley in 1968. The Evertonians were ecstatic. Two trips to Wembley in one season was more than they could have ever dreamed of, only this time they were determined to see their beloved Everton win.

Above: *A jubilant Adrian Heath celebrates his FA Cup semi-final winner in 1984 against Southampton.*

Opposite: *The final whistle blows at Highbury after Everton's FA Cup semi-final victory over Southampton, 1984. Colin Harvey explodes with excitement. Everton boss Howard Kendall retained his composure until he got to the sanctuary of the players' tunnel. Photographer Steve Hale recalls: 'Howard held back his emotions until he got to the tunnel and then began punching the air, shouting "Yes! We've done it!"'*

Southampton Manager Laurie McMenemy told the press afterwards that Everton looked so confident before the game that he never really expected his team to triumph. He said: 'I looked round my dressing-room before the start and these were experienced players looking anxious and nervous. I watched Everton run out and there wasn't a nerve amongst them, so I feared the worst.' Adrian Heath had little doubt about the reasons behind Everton's self-confidence and the two players who instilled belief in the whole team – Andy Gray and Peter Reid. Heath recalled: 'We signed Peter Reid and Andy Gray and they gave us a belief that we were good. They would come in at half-time effing and blinding. Reidy instilled belief in us by example. It was more in the way that he played. Andy was more vocal. He would say: "If we're not going to do this we may as well pack it in now." The two of them would be screaming and shouting, "Right lads! Let's get out there and get stuck into them and sort them out." A few of the younger ones in the team amongst us thought: "Right, this is the way you must have to play if you want to be successful."' Not bringing the FA Cup back to Goodison was never contemplated by anyone at Everton in 1984. They would have Peter Reid, and the more frightening prospect of Andy Gray to answer to if they failed.

Adrian Heath proudly displays the Steve Hale photograph that captured his FA Cup semi-final winner against Southampton.

Everton's opponents at Wembley were first-time finalists Watford. The London club, managed by the up-and-coming new kid on the managerial block, Graham Taylor, looked to be a club going places. Rock star Elton John was club chairman and they also had the future Anfield legend John Barnes in attack. Watford were not expected to be a pushover. They had finished the season in mid-table just five points behind Everton, so a tight game was expected. Before the game Andy Gray had given his usual pep talk, telling his team-mates that: 'If I hear anyone saying it's going to be a nice day out, I'm going to knock them out.' Gray reasoned that it wouldn't be a nice day for the team if they did not return to Merseyside with the cup. After Graeme Sharp had scored the first goal, followed in the second-half by a controversial Andy Gray effort, when he appeared to head the ball out of the Watford goalkeeper Steve Sherwood's hands as he came out to claim a cross, the FA Cup returned to Everton for the first time in eighteen years.

Everton had obtained rich consolation for their Milk Cup defeat against Liverpool two months earlier. The blue half of Merseyside was ecstatic. Young central defender Derek Mountfield had supported the Goodison Park club all his life, and now to be a part of an Everton FA Cup-winning team was a dream come true. Reflecting on the day he said:

Peter Reid in action against Watford in the 1984 FA Cup final.

Andy Gray celebrates after scoring against Watford in the 1984 FA Cup final. Goals from Gray and Sharp gave Everton a 2-0 victory. The FA Cup was back at Goodison for the first time since 1966.

Left: *Boyhood Evertonian, Derek Mountfield, proudly displays the FA Cup, 1984.*

Below: *The Everton team celebrate their comprehensive FA Cup final victory over Watford, 1984. From left to right, back row: Mountfield, Bailey, Reid, Harper, Gray. Front row: Steven Richardson, Southall, Ratcliffe, Sharp, Heath, Stevens.*

Opposite: *The Everton team on their homecoming tour of Liverpool after their FA Cup victory, 1984.*

'The whole of the final was like a dream. It was over so quickly that it had gone before I realised it. I remember Elton John came out onto the pitch and wished us all a good game as he shook us by the hand. After the final whistle went I was carried away and couldn't remember anything about the game until I watched it on TV later that evening. When we reached Wembley before the game I do remember being surrounded by a sea of blue and white. It meant so much to the Evertonians.'

Most of the following day's newspapers heaped praise on both teams for what had been an entertaining final. Singled out for a special plaudit was the Everton goalkeeper, Neville Southall. *The Daily Telegraph* correspondent remarked: 'But for the brilliance of Southall in goal, Watford would have made much more of a game of it.' Southall, like the majority of the Everton team, was developing into an outstanding player. Howard Kendall told the press that he had few doubts about Southall's ability, claiming: 'Neville had a bit of a shaky start at Everton but I never had any doubts that he would become a great goalkeeper.' Just how great Southall was destined to become would be manifested the following season, when he would be widely acclaimed as one of, if not the, best, goalkeepers in the world. As for the Everton team who had looked likely relegation candidates just five months earlier, by the end of the following 1984/85 season they would be talked of as possibly the best team in Europe.

From left to right: Adrian Heath, Mark Higgins, Gary Stevens and Colin Harvey training at Bellefield.

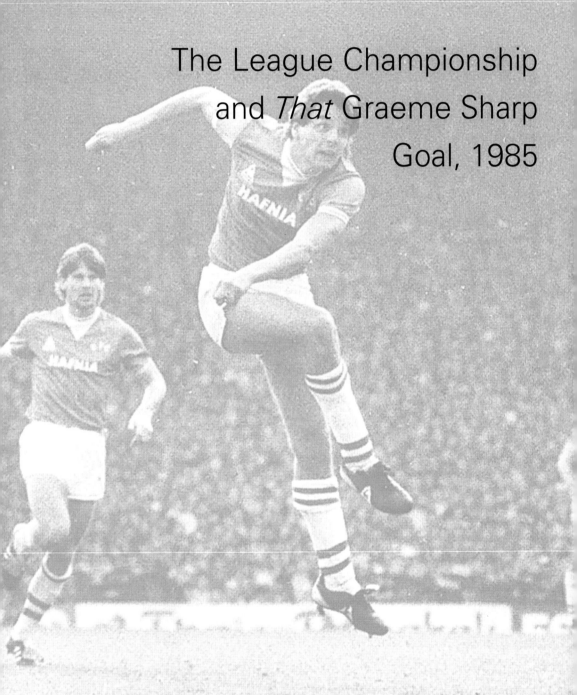

six

The League Championship and *That* Graeme Sharp Goal, 1985

Graeme Sharp scores with a fantastic volley against Liverpool at Anfield in October 1984. Sharp's goal gave Everton a 1-0 victory and was selected as the BBC's 'Goal of the Season'. Liverpool boss, Joe Fagan, said after the game: 'It was a bloody good goal, worth winning any game.'

'The Everton side of the mid-1980s was the best side in which I ever played. When we stood in the tunnel waiting to run out onto the pitch at Goodison Park we just knew we were going to win.'

Andy Gray

The season of 1984/85 was the greatest in Everton's history. Unbelievably they began the campaign with a 4-1 defeat at home to Spurs, followed by an away loss at West Brom. After their shaky start they returned to form with 10 victories in their next 13 games. And, as if Everton did not already have an abundance of players with a touch of steel about them, they added one of the hardest defenders in the League to their team, Pat Van den Hauwe. Van den Hauwe, soon to be dubbed 'Psycho-Pat' by some of the Goodison regulars, joined another exceptional newcomer in Paul Bracewell, who had been signed from Sunderland during the summer break. Both would improve their game greatly after joining the Everton ranks and become players of international class. Never afraid to gamble when it came to signing players who may have had injury problems hanging over them in the past, such as Reid and Gray, Howard Kendall was also not shy about taking the odd player with a hell-raising reputation either. Talking about the signing of Van den Hauwe, Kevin Ratcliffe remarked: 'There were a few managers who wouldn't have touched Pat Van den Hauwe. But the gamble certainly paid off. Pat gave us extra steel and pace.'

With Ratcliffe, Stevens, Mountfield and now Van den Hauwe, Everton certainly possessed one of the most mobile back fours in the League. All were remarkably fit defenders whose powers of recovery were phenomenal. Recalling his days being marked by his friend and Welsh team-mate, Ian Rush said of Ratcliffe: 'I'd much rather face the so-called hard man type of defender than the pacy ones like Kevin Ratcliffe.' And as to Pat Van den Hauwe's reputation as one of the toughest defenders of the 1980s, was it justified? Former Everton and Liverpool midfield enforcer, Steve McMahon, had no doubts. McMahon claimed: 'Pat Van den Hauwe is a one-off. Off the pitch he is not a bad lad when you get to know him. But on the pitch something can just snap. I remember his derby match tackle on Craig Johnston. It was enough to dissuade Craig from taking any liberties during the rest of the match.' Pat Van den Hauwe had made just two League appearances in the Everton team when he was thrust into the red-hot cauldron of a Merseyside derby. It was during this game that a goal was scored that Evertonians never tire of seeing repeated whenever derby day comes around again. The

Graeme Sharp celebrates after his stunning goal against Liverpool, 1984.

20 October 1984 was the day that Graeme Sharp scored the goal that has gone down into the annals of Everton folklore.

It is probably surpassed by just two: the legendary 'Dixie' Dean's 60th League goal of the season in 1928 that set an English goalscoring record that will never be broken, and Derek Temple's 1966 FA Cup final winner against Sheffield Wednesday that brought the trophy back to Goodison for the first time since the 1930s. When Graeme Sharp hit a thirty-yard volley past the incredulous Bruce Grobbelaar in the Liverpool goal, it was as if in that instant Everton had finally broken free from living in the shadows of their Anfield rivals. They had not won at Anfield for fourteen years; they had not won the League Championship since 1970. When that Sharp goal hit the back of the net, Evertonians and the millions watching on live television knew they were witnessing a balance of power shift between the two Merseyside giants. Everton's 1-0 victory confirmed what most of football already knew. They were now a major force in English football again.

Peter Reid, recalling their momentous Anfield victory in later years, said: 'Graeme's goal was probably the best of the lot. I got the ball and laid it to Gary Stevens and he hit a long ball forward to Graeme. He got a lovely touch over Hansen and volleyed it past Grobbelaar – and the Anfield Road End, where the Evertonians were gathered, exploded. Everton were really up for it that day.' Sharp's goal went on to become

Just a week after their crucial derby victory over Liverpool, Everton returned to Goodison and trounced Manchester United 5-0 in October 1984. Adrian Heath can be seen here scoring the third of Everton's goals. Kevin Sheedy, who needed stitches in a head wound, can also be seen.

Kevin Sheedy scores Everton's second against Manchester United. Sheedy scored two in Everton's 5-0 victory.

Above: *Derek Mountfield almost converts another chance in Everton's magnificent 5-0 victory over Manchester United, 1984.*

Opposite: *Reid, Stevens and Mountfield celebrate their 5-0 drubbing of Manchester United in 1984. Former Goodison great, Joe Mercer, witnessed Everton's display from the stands. After the game he said it was the greatest performance that he had ever seen by an Everton team. Evertonians were now confident that after this display the League Championship trophy would soon be back at Goodison Park.*

selected as the BBC 'Goal of the Season' and the Liverpool manager at the time, Joe Fagan, acknowledged: 'It was a bloody good goal, worth winning any game. It would almost have been a shame for us to score after a goal like that.'

Everton's new signing, Paul Bracewell, also believed that the Sharp goal was a seminal moment in Everton's history when he recalled: 'I made my Everton debut when we beat Liverpool in the Charity Shield at Wembley in 1984. But the victory over Liverpool that gave me the most pleasure was when Graeme Sharp scored the only goal of the game at Anfield. That really made people believe we could win the Championship.'

Within a short space of time, Paul Bracewell settled into the Everton midfield as though he had been a part of the Goodison set up for years. His midfield partner, Peter Reid, admitted that he had his reservations when Kendall first signed the Sunderland midfielder, but these soon vanished. Reid said: 'I remember thinking when he bought Paul Bracewell that he might be too similar to me. But it worked. We were both tacklers, getting the ball and giving it, engine-room players. We stayed solid in the middle and left Trevor Steven and Kevin Sheedy to get on with it out wide.'

Everton's derby victory was followed a week later by an astonishing 5-0 demolition of Manchester United at Goodison. The Blues were simply scintillating that October day and were now playing with a style and a swagger that Evertonians had not witnessed since the days of the outstanding 1969/70 team. Goals were flowing from every section of the team, and even central-defender Derek Mountfield weighed in during the campaign with ten League goals. When Everton beat Newcastle 4-0 at Goodison at the

beginning of January 1985, they went to the top of the League and stayed there until the end of the season.

Everton's success had been built on a superb team effort from the manager Howard Kendall, first-team coaches Colin Harvey and Mick Heaton, and an outstanding squad of players. Two of the team, Neville Southall and Peter Reid, were singled out for special acclaim when Southall was voted 'Footballer of the Year' and Reid the 'Players' Player of the Year.' Manager Kendall was also awarded the 'Manager of the Year' accolade.

Everton Football Club have had many fine goalkeepers throughout their history, most notably Gordon West in the 1960s and the legendary Ted Sagar during the 1930s and post-war period. But there have been none at Goodison Park to equal Southall, before or since. The idiosyncratic keeper prepared for games in his own way and would argue his point with anyone if he thought he was in the right. After one game, Kendall was having a go at Southall for straying too far off his line to intercept a cross. Neville never made it and it cost Everton a goal. After his manager had made his point, Southall shrugged his shoulders and said: 'Alright, if you're that worried about me coming off the line, why don't you buy some rope and tie me to the posts!' Howard Kendall was also keen on taking his team out as a unit for a meal and a plentiful quantity of beer several times a year. Southall would go along with his boss's team-building routine, but would never indulge in the alcohol on offer, preferring several pots of tea instead. As a goalkeeper Southall had few peers, and former England great Gordon Banks recalled the keeper's power and ability: 'In the 1980s Neville Southall was the best keeper in the world. His reflexes are like lightning and he's so powerful. I used to coach him once a week at Everton using a medicine ball; when he threw it back he used to knock me over with it.'

Opposite: *On the verge of the England squad, Everton's Adrian Heath is badly injured by a Brian Marwood tackle playing against Sheffield Wednesday at Goodison. The injury Heath sustained resulted in him missing out on the rest of Everton's historic 1984/85 season.*

Above: *The badly injured Adrian Heath is helped off by team-mates during the Everton v. Sheffield Wednesday match, 1984.*

Right: *Adrian Heath rests his injured foot in a bucket. The injury would cost him dearly.*

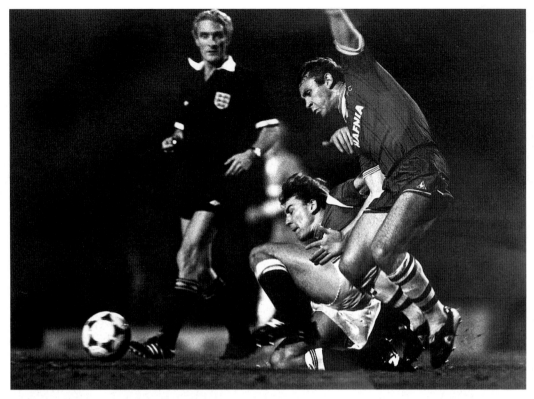

England team-mates Peter Reid and Bryan Robson tangle at Old Trafford in a third round Milk Cup-tie, 1984. Everton won 2-1.

Kevin Sheedy in action against Grimsby Town in a fourth round Milk Cup-tie, 1984. Grimsby surprisingly knocked Everton out of the competition with a 1-0 victory at Goodison.

Derek Mountfield scores for Everton in their 1-1 draw in the League at Old Trafford, 1985. Everton went on to win the title ahead of Liverpool, Spurs and Manchester United.

Team-mate Andy Gray also had no doubts that Southall was the best: 'Neville is the complete keeper. He is brave, agile, has unbelievably quick reflexes and he's intimidating. He has great physical strength and some of his saves have to be seen to be believed.'

The outstanding shot-stopping ability of Southall was reckoned to have been worth ten points or more to Everton during their two title-winning campaigns of the 1980s. When he was informed that he had been selected as 'Footballer of the Year', the modest Southall said that it was a proud moment, but that he was surprised to have become the first Everton player to have won it. He remarked: 'When you consider some of the fabulous Everton players there have been over the years, I was amazed to be told I was the first player from the club to have won the award.' When asked if he recalled any particular saves that stood out for him during the title-winning season, he said:

> 'One that stands out from the others came against QPR. It was a Bank Holiday Monday and a 50,000-plus crowd were willing us to the title. In an evenly

matched game, Mark Falco was put clear through. A goal looked a certainty, but somehow I managed to make as important a save as I'd ever made. We won the game and went on to take the title.'

'Players' Player of the Year' Peter Reid was overjoyed at his accolade. Former Goodison favourite Terry Darracott said of Reid: 'He was a great player because the bottle the lad's got is unbelievable. He set an example at Everton to the young players. He never stopped running, never stopped tackling.' Howard Kendall remarked: 'Peter Reid is like Star Trek. He boldly goes where no man has gone before.' Peter Reid himself put Everton's remarkable 1984/85 season down to the tremendous team spirit and squad at Goodison. 'Everton's secret was the squad players like Kevin Richardson and Alan Harper coming in and doing a job, Pat Van den Hauwe when he arrived from Birmingham, Andy Gray taking over where 'Inchy' left off. Everybody gave something.'

Above: *Andy Gray celebrates Everton's Championship victory, 1985.*

Opposite: *Everton's midfield tigers, Paul Bracewell (left) and Peter Reid patrol the park in a 1980s encounter.*

Left: *Everton captain Kevin Ratcliffe holds the First Division Championship trophy aloft, 1985.*

Below: *Peter Reid celebrates Everton's 1985 Championship victory with Adrian Heath. Injury robbed Heath of playing a role in the second half of the 1984/85 campaign.*

Opposite above: *Derek Mountfield, Pat Van den Hauwe and Andy Gray parade the Championship trophy around Goodison Park, 1985.*

Opposite below: *Everton manager Howard Kendall celebrates Everton's Championship success with Paul Bracewell, 1985.*

Sheedy, Stevens, Steven, Sharp, Ratcliffe and Southall celebrate at Goodison after Everton's Championship victory, 1985.

The Everton Championship-winning team parade around Goodison, 1985.

The Goodison glory boys with the League Championship trophy, 1985. From left to right, back row: Bracewell, Atkins, Van den Hauwe, Gray, Stevens, Southall, Mountfield. Front row: Reid, Richardson, Sheedy, Sharp, Ratcliffe, Steven.

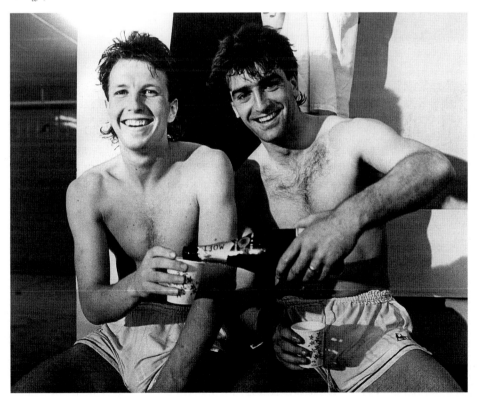

Trevor Steven and Kevin Ratcliffe toast Everton's great Championship victory with champagne, 1985.

Above left: *Howard Kendall holds the First Division Championship trophy, 1985.*

Above right: *The great Neville Southall, voted 'Footballer of the Year'. He was the first Everton player to receive this accolade.*

Left: *Howard Kendall wins another Bell's 'Manager of the Month' award during the 1984/85 season.*

seven

From Dublin to Rotterdam: The European Cup Winners' Cup, 1985

Adrian Heath scores against Inter Bratislava in the second round of the European Cup Winners' Cup at Goodison Park, 1984. Goals from Heath, Sharp and Sheedy gave Everton a 3-0 victory. They went through to the next round 4-0 on aggregate.

'Our team could not withstand it. We could not live with Everton.'

Otto Baric, Rapid Vienna coach

The story of Everton's trophy-winning European campaign began in Dublin against the part-timers of UCD (University College Dublin) on 19 September 1984. The Dublin club surprised Everton, holding them to a 0-0 draw in the first leg. In the return game, only a single strike from Graeme Sharp gave Everton a scrappy 1-0 victory. They hardly looked like potential winners of the cup, but would improve dramatically as the competition progressed. Next up for Everton was Inter Bratislava of Czechoslovakia. A Paul Bracewell goal gave the Blues a comfortable victory in the away leg against a Czech side that hardly had a shot on goal. Goals from Sharp, Sheedy and Heath in the home game eased Everton into the next round, where they would play Fortuna Sittard of Holland. Howard Kendall was pleased at the way his team had adapted to European competition, which needed a more measured approach than the domestic game. In the home leg against Fortuna Andy Gray was sensational, knocking in a hat-trick in a 3-0 victory. Gray did not play in the away game, but goals from Reid and Sharp took Everton into the semi-finals, where probably the greatest test that they had ever encountered in Europe awaited them – the might of Germany in the shape of Bayern Munich.

Howard Kendall once said that the European Cup Winners' Cup semi-finals against Bayern Munich were really the final. They were by far the two best teams left in the competition and whoever triumphed in the semis would be odds on favourites to win the final. Everton put up an outstanding performance to hold Bayern to a 0-0 draw in the away game at Munich's Olympic Stadium, the Blues maintaining their record of not conceding a goal in the competition so far. But the Germans, who had disposed of Italian giants Roma in the previous round, were confident that they could come to Goodison and win. The return game against Bayern has gone down in Goodison Park legend as probably the greatest post-war match that has ever been played on the ground. Evertonians had never had much to be proud of when it came to their club's record in European competitions, but this was all about to change in dramatic fashion.

Anticipation was high before the game that Everton would reach their first ever European final. Photographer Steve Hale recalls that the atmosphere at the ground that momentous night was something that he had never experienced before or since. Steve said:

Above: *Andy Gray scored a sensational hat-trick during Everton's 3-0 home victory over Fortuna Sittard of Holland in the quarter-finals of the 1985 European Cup Winners' Cup. Here, Gray can be seen diving in on the Fortuna goal. Gray was rested for the return leg, but Everton still managed a 2-0 victory to go through to the semi-finals 5-0 on aggregate.*

Opposite above: *Terry Curran celebrates with Andy Gray after Gray scores against Fortuna Sittard, 1985.*

Opposite below: *Andy Gray scores against Fortuna Sittard, 1985.*

'I remember that Goodison Park was packed to the rafters hours before the kick-off. There seemed to be an air of expectancy as if the Evertonians sensed that they were about to witness something special. As things turned out they were present, in my opinion, at the greatest night in the club's history. It has gone down into the annals of Merseyside football folklore.'

The Everton team and their fans knew that defeating Bayern would not be easy, and when Hoeness gave the Germans a 1-0 lead at half-time, their hopes of a first European final appeared to be slipping away.

From all accounts, Howard Kendall told his team during the interval to keep knocking the ball high to Andy Gray and Graeme Sharp: 'They're frightened to death of Sharpy and Andy in the air. Put them under pressure and the Gwladys Street End will suck the

Above: *Graeme Sharp equalises against Bayern Munich in the European Cup Winners' Cup semi-final at Goodison Park, 1985. In one of the greatest nights in Everton's history, goals from Sharp, Gray and Steven took Everton through to their first European final 3-1 on aggregate.*

Opposite above: *Andy Gray celebrates his goal against Bayern Munich.*

Opposite below: *Trevor Steven clinches Everton's European Cup Winners' Cup final place with the third goal against Bayern Munich 1985.*

ball into the net', was the Everton boss's assessment. His players did just that and in the second-half Bayern literally did not know what had hit them. Roared on by 50,000 delirious fans, Everton tore into the German team from the start of resumption of play. The gladiatorial Andy Gray was putting on an exhibition of aggressive centre forward play that had not been seen at Goodison since the days of Dave Hickson in his pomp. Recalling the game, Neville Southall remarked: 'Andy basically bulldozed his way through everybody on the pitch. If we hadn't had Andy we may have lost the game. Once he'd flattened a few people they just put the white flag up. Everyone was prepared to die to get through.' Everton's pressure paid off and Sharp equalised, followed by goals from Gray and Trevor Steven. Before the game, Everton were already building a name throughout Europe as a team to be feared. When news of their demolition of the outstanding Bayern Munich team spread, they were being widely touted as one of the favourites for the following season's European Cup. At the end of the Bayern game Andy Gray was approached by the German club's manager who started shouting at the startled Scot. 'He was pointing his fingers and jumping up and down, saying: "You, you are a crazy man",' recalled Gray, 'It might have had something to do with the fact that the player who had been marking me had had his nose broken in two places.'

Everton were through to their first European final and their opponents were Austria's Rapid Vienna. The game was played in Rotterdam on 15 May 1985, and after winning the League Championship, the European Cup Winners' Cup would hopefully be the second leg of a unique treble of major trophies for the Blues. Just four days after the Cup Winners' Cup final, Everton would play Manchester United at Wembley in the FA Cup final. The atmosphere before the final between the Everton and Rapid fans was friendly. Supporters mingled together in the bars and streets of the Town Square, exchanging scarves, with games of street football springing up between the opposing supporters and even the Dutch police. It was estimated that over 25,000 Evertonians had made the trip and confidence was high that they would return with the trophy. Howard Kendall had watched Rapid play before the final and it had confirmed to him that the Austrians were not in the same class as Bayern Munich. In Hans Krankl they had a striker who had been world-class at his best, but he was now reaching the end of his distinguished career.

An Everton victory was expected and Kendall and his team were confident. The Rapid Vienna coach had stated before the game that his team would attack Everton from the kick-off, but they never got the opportunity. Everton stroked the ball about for the opening quarter, and then gradually began to put the pressure on the Austrians. High crosses to Gray and Sharp had Vienna in trouble. Mountfield nodded a Sheedy cross down to Gray, who thought he had scored, but it was disallowed for offside. It was obvious for all to see that it would be only a matter of time before Everton would make the breakthrough, and the first goal came in the fifty-seventh minute. Everton's pressure paid off and Sharp equalised, followed by goals from Gray and Trevor Steven. Graeme Sharp chipped the ball across the Rapid goal for Gray to hit the back of the net from just eight yards out. The Everton onslaught was unabating and Trevor Steven smashed the ball home from a Sheedy corner to make it 2-0. The veteran Hans Krankl pulled one back for Rapid, before Sheedy scored with a brilliant twenty-five yard drive to enable Everton to coast to a comfortable 3-1 victory. Everton had won in Europe for the first time. Rotterdam was a sea of blue and white as Everton fans celebrated their team's brilliant victory. A shell-shocked Rapid Vienna coach, Otto Baric, said after the game: 'Our team could not withstand it. We could not live with Everton.' Hans Krankl congratulated his team's English conquerors and declared: 'I can't remember the last time I played against a team as good as Everton. They were far too good for us. In most European games you are generally given a chance to win at some time in the match. They gave us no chance. They had so many attacking options that we never knew what hit us. English sides always give you a chance, but not Everton.'

Everton's jubilant captain, Kevin Ratcliffe, told the press: 'I think we surprised them because they expected us to come at them from the start like we did against Bayern Munich. But we played the ball about. The lads were really keyed up, but we couldn't help playing well with a crowd like that behind us. The fans were fantastic. The whole ground was a sea of blue and white. They seemed to outnumber the Vienna supporters by about five to one. I've never seen anything like it.' Goalscoring hero Kevin Sheedy spoke about missing out on moments like these during his Anfield days and reflected: 'I was in the background at Liverpool and never felt a part of it when the team were winning things. Now I know what it feels like to go out and be involved in winning a European final. No words can describe it.' Peter Reid, after another dynamic display in midfield, told *The Liverpool Echo*: 'That's our best performance of the season. It's a joy to play in the current Everton team. Everyone plays for each other. We seem to be getting

Evertonians prepare for the 1985 European Cup Winners' Cup final in Rotterdam against Rapid Vienna. Note that some are wearing the new Everton shirts that the team did not play in until the following season.

Above: *The atmosphere builds before the 1985 European Cup Winners' Cup final.*

Opposite: *An anxious-looking Everton bench before the start of the 1985 European Cup Winners' Cup final. Howard Kendall was confident after they had beaten Bayern Munich in the semi-finals that Everton would win the trophy.*

better and better.' Howard Kendall had achieved the distinction of becoming the first
Everton boss to taste European glory. A delighted Kendall said:

> 'It's a tribute to the quality of the players and the efforts of the backroom staff that
> we have marched straight through to our first European trophy. We never let
> Rapid settle or gain confidence. It was total domination, an occasion I will always
> savour. Our team set an example in terms of football and our 25,000 fans set an
> example in terms of behaviour.'

The fine behaviour of the Evertonians was applauded not just throughout Rotterdam,
but on the ferries transporting the fans to the final. On one of the numerous boats
returning to Britain the captain made a special announcement over the ship's Tannoy
system to proclaim: 'You've been ambassadors for British football. Thank you Everton
and your fans.'

Trevor Steven glides past another tackle as he attacks the Rapid goal.

Above: *Andy Gray blasts the ball into the Rapid Vienna net to open the scoring for Everton. Further goals from Steven and Sheedy gave Everton a comfortable 3-1 victory.*

Right: *Andy Gray celebrates his goal against Rapid Vienna with Peter Reid, Graeme Sharp and Paul Bracewell.*

Left: *Neville Southall holds the European Cup Winners' Cup trophy aloft after Everton's great victory in the final.*

Below: *The Everton team that won the European Cup Winners' Cup in 1985. Was this the greatest team in Everton's history? Many Evertonians think so. From left to right, back row: Atkins, Van den Hauwe, Harper, Gray, Arnold, Southall, Mountfield, Bailey, Bracewell. Front row: Richardson, Sheedy, Ratcliffe, Sharp, Steven, Reid. Not in the photograph are Gary Stevens, who played in the final, and the injured Adrian Heath.*

Right: *A jubilant Peter Reid with the European Cup Winners' Cup, 1985.*

Below: *The League Champions and European Cup Winners' Cup winners, 1985. Everton parade through the streets of Liverpool during their homecoming celebrations.*

Above: *The Everton homecoming celebrations, 1985.*

Left: *Everton captain, Kevin Ratcliffe, proudly displays Everton's trophy haul before the start of the 1985/86 season.*

eight

The Double
Fantasy, 1985

Andy Gray displays great courage to dive in where the boots are flying during Everton's 1985 FA Cup-tie against Doncaster Rovers. Everton won the fourth round tie 2-0.

'More than anything we wanted the League and Cup double, but our bodies wouldn't respond. Within minutes of the FA Cup final kicking off, we realised just how much the European final had taken out of us.'

Andy Gray

Everton's defence of the FA Cup started in the third round in a televised Friday night game at Leeds United. Despite a bone-hard frozen pitch, Everton's class enabled them to reach the next round without too much trouble, Sharp and Sheedy scoring the goals. It was Yorkshire opposition again in the fourth round in the shape of Doncaster Rovers at Goodison. Goals from Trevor Steven and Gary Stevens put Everton through to face non-League Telford next. As usual, Howard Kendall watched Everton's next opponents in action himself, and his conclusion was that Telford were the best non-League side that he had seen. As expected, Telford put up a brave display, but the huge gulf in class told in the final quarter and goals from Reid, Sheedy and Steven saw Everton run out 3-0 winners.

Ipswich in the quarter-finals provided a much sterner test and it was only due to their indomitable fighting spirit that Everton managed to scrape a 2-2 draw in the first game at Goodison. Ipswich went into the lead, but Everton, through the magic left foot of Kevin Sheedy from a twice taken free-kick, equalised. Sheedy bent his first effort over the Ipswich wall and past Cooper's right for a sensational goal. Goodison erupted, only for the referee to disallow it because he had not blown for the kick to be taken. The ice-cool Sheedy then put the ball back on the same spot, ran up and placed the ball with maximum precision past the startled Ipswich keeper on his left-hand side. Kevin Sheedy was renowned throughout his Everton career for his ability at taking free-kicks, but it is doubtful if any surpassed this particular gem. Ipswich, who were a dogged outfit, fought back to take a 2-1 lead at the interval. Everton pinned Ipswich back into their own half with continuous pressure in the second half but the Blues looked to be heading out of the FA Cup with the Ipswich defence led by Terry Butcher holding firm. The minutes were ticking by when defender Derek Mountfield, who was having an outstanding season at Goodison, popped up with a headed equaliser. Everton have not had a central defender before or since the days of Mountfield with such an uncanny knack of scoring vital goals on such a regular basis. Mountfield's last-gasp equaliser took Everton to a replay at Portman Road, where a Graeme Sharp penalty put the Blues into the semi-finals.

Above: *Graeme Sharp is ready to pounce during the 1985 FA Cup-tie against Doncaster Rovers. Goals from Steven and Stevens won the game for Everton.*

Opposite: *Trevor Steven takes on a Telford defender during Everton's fifth round FA Cup-tie against the non-League team. Goals from Reid, Sheedy and Steven gave Everton a 3-0 victory.*

Everton's semi-final opponents were Luton Town at Villa Park. Looking jaded from their mid-week European Cup Winners' Cup game against Bayern Munich in Germany, Everton started slowly and Luton seized the initiative with a Ricky Hill goal in the first-half. With their never-say-die fighting spirit that Everton became noted for during their golden period of the mid-1980s, a Sheedy free-kick levelled the game with just minutes remaining. With Everton almost certain of taking the League title to Goodison, the prospect of a first-ever League and Cup double was still on. In extra-time, with Everton dominating the tiring Luton team, Derek Mountfield made his way into the opposition penalty area to head a Sheedy cross past Les Sealey. Everton were through to yet another Wembley final, where their opponents would be Manchester United. Optimism was high that the double was coming to Goodison. Everton had already hammered United 5-0 earlier in the season and Ron Atkinson's team trailed the Blues by fourteen points in fourth spot after the final League games of the season.

After Everton's triumph in Europe against Rapid Vienna in the final of the European Cup Winners' Cup, they were confident that not just the domestic double, but an unprecedented treble could be achieved. After their mid-week exertions Everton were bound to feel a little leg-weary, but United had also played a League game just a few days before the final. At the end of a hard season both teams were bound to have diminished energy levels, but the fact that the game was played on such a warm May afternoon appeared to hit Everton harder than it did Manchester United. Everton's play lacked the zip and quality that they had displayed just days earlier against Rapid Vienna.

Above: *Andy Gray in action against Telford, FA Cup 1985. Howard Kendall described Telford as the best non-League team that he had ever seen.*

Opposite: *Derek Mountfield pops up to score Everton's equaliser in the 1985 FA Cup quarter-final tie against Ipswich at Goodison. Mountfield's goal gave Everton a 2-2 draw. There has not been a central defender before or since Mountfield at Everton who had this uncanny knack of scoring vital goals for the club.*

The first ninety minutes of the 1985 FA Cup final failed to produce a winner and, apart from the sensational first-ever dismissal in an FA Cup final, it was not a game that lingered long in the memory.

The extra-time sending off of United's Kevin Moran was expected to hand the initiative to Everton, but it was Manchester United who suddenly lifted their game. United's Viv Anderson, recalling the incident that saw Moran sent off for a professional foul on Peter Reid, said:

'The turning point was the ordering off of Kevin Moran for an innocuous tackle. He should never have gone. Suddenly the referee was ordering Kevin off. It was the ref's last game before he retired. He decided to make the headlines, and it could have ruined the game, but instead the match caught fire because all of us were so upset at what happened.'

Moran himself, speaking recently about referee Peter Willis sending him off, said: 'I remember Andy Gray shouting "Send him off ref! Send him off!" When the ref did,

Andy said to me as I trouped past him, "Well, I didn't expect that!" Everton were now obvious favourites to go on and win, but it was United who lifted their game. They suddenly had renewed energy and Everton were almost out on their feet. It was no surprise when Norman Whiteside burst down the right, leaving Pat Van den Hauwe in his wake and curled a sensational winner past the diving Southall. The galvanised Manchester United team held on for a famous victory and the Everton dream of the Treble was over.

Everton's success during the 1980s was built on superb fitness and superiority over the opposition when it came to strength and determination, but this was one occasion when it deserted them. Many Evertonians feel that if the final had been played the following Saturday, allowing Everton to recover from their European exertions, then the Blues would have beaten United. Their team appeared to have come out at Wembley physically and emotionally drained. But all of this is conjecture and the record books show that Manchester United took the FA Cup back to Old Trafford in 1985.

Above: *Andy Gray has a goal disallowed in the FA Cup-tie against Ipswich, 1985. Everton won the replay 1-0 through a Sharp goal.*

Opposite: *Derek Mountfield celebrates his FA Cup equaliser against Ipswich, 1985. A dejected Terry Butcher and George Burley look on in disbelief.*

They may have been denied the Treble, but Everton had shown during 1984/85 that they were now one of the most formidable teams in Europe. They looked forward with confidence to the following season when they would be competing in the European Cup for the first time since the 1970/71 season. But their dreams of glory in Europe's greatest club competition were brought to a shattering halt when the events at Heysel led to severe repercussions for all English clubs. Everton's European aspirations would have to be put on hold for the foreseeable future. A dejected Andy Gray voiced the feelings of himself and his team-mates when he remarked: 'Having clinched the League, while we were waiting for the Heysel game to take place, all our talk was of "We hope Liverpool win the European Cup and that we can play them in the European Cup final next year." That was what we were looking for, and the opportunity was denied us.' Kevin Ratcliffe on the same subject, said:

> 'People still believe we would have won the European Cup the following season. Of course you can't prove anything, but I feel we were good enough to have at least made the semi-finals. As it was, the blanket ban on English teams in Europe meant the team fell apart. We were denied the chance to pit ourselves against the best in Europe.'

Neville Southall, however, had no doubt that Everton would have swept all before them the following season. He remarked: 'That Everton team was exceptional. Under Howard Kendall I am convinced that we would have won the European Cup.'

Above: *A disbelieving Kevin Moran becomes the first player to be sent off in an FA Cup final after fouling Peter Reid. Manchester United went on to win the 1985 final 1-0 in extra time, Norman Whiteside scoring the goal. United's Frank Stapleton can be seen consoling Moran. The referee is Peter Willes.*

Opposite: *Kevin Sheedy's shot beats the Luton Town goalkeeper in the FA Cup semi-final tie at Villa Park, 1985. Everton won 2-1, Derek Mountfield scoring the winner.*

Left: *Everton's Peter Reid consoles Kevin Moran after the Manchester United defender was sent off in the 1985 FA Cup final.*

Below: *Manchester United manager Ron Atkinson consoles the Everton players after his team had just beaten them in the 1985 FA Cup final.*

nine

So Near and
Yet So Far, 1986

The Merseyside derby of September 1985 resulted in a 3-2 defeat for Everton. Here, former Blue Steve McMahon can be seen scoring Liverpool's third goal.

'The Everton side of 1985/86 was the best club team I ever played in. We should have won the double that year.'

Gary Lineker

With the Heysel tragedy putting an end to Everton's dream of competing in the European Cup, the club set about retaining their League title with some dramatic pre-season transfer activity. After just two seasons at the club, Andy Gray was sold to Aston Villa. He didn't want to leave but Everton were keen to bring Leicester's Gary Lineker to Goodison and with Adrian Heath waiting in the wings to return after injury there would soon be a surplus of goalscorers at Goodison. Graeme Sharp was by now probably the most complete centre forward in the English game and it was unlikely that he would make way for Lineker. Ian Rush was once asked if he could have any player in the world game to play alongside, who would it be? Without a moment's hesitation he replied 'Graeme Sharp.' So it was Lineker in and Andy Gray out. Gray spoke with pride about his momentous couple of seasons at Everton when he said: 'I suppose I was a little hurt by the way the Everton manager had cast me off, that's football though. Everton was, and still is a great club and wherever I go I'll be proud to say I was once part of it.' Evertonians just wished that Gray had arrived at Goodison ten years earlier in his career.

Andy Gray will never be forgotten at Goodison, neither will the goalscoring legend of the future who was about to take his place. Gary Lineker was at Everton for just one season, but what a season it was.

When he first joined the club there was still a certain amount of animosity shown to him from the pro-Andy Gray Evertonians at Goodison. It took him four games to score his first goal for the Blues, but after that he never stopped scoring. Lineker's first goal at Spurs was followed a few days later with a hat-trick against Birmingham. Lineker then scored two more in a 5-1 win at Sheffield Wednesday. After a poor start, Everton, inspired by Linkeker's goalscoring exploits, had won three League games on the trot. An overjoyed Gary Lineker told the press: 'I always wanted to play for a big club. I knew I could keep scoring goals. Leaving Leicester was a wrench and it was a bit awkward at first. There was a small faction at Everton who would have preferred to have had Andy Gray still in the team. It wasn't easy trying to fit in with different players, but it's getting better every game.' Howard Kendall was delighted with his new £800,000 acquisition and said: 'Gary has scored six goals in three games. Not bad is it? He has so much pace

The new Everton home and away strip, modelled here by Kevin Ratcliffe and Gary Stevens before the start of the 1985/86 campaign. The Everton bib shirt was only used for one season.

and an extraordinary ability to get in between defenders. I think he is going to be really spectacular for Everton.'

Lineker did prove to be spectacular for the Blues as he gelled with Graeme Sharp to provide a fearsome combination up front. By the time his second derby game arrived in February 1986, Everton had clawed back Manchester United's early season lead when they looked to be running away with the League. Lineker had scored in his first derby at Goodison, but Liverpool had run out 3-2 winners in one of the best games between the two sides in years. Everton were out for revenge and also to keep in contention with Manchester United and Liverpool in the race for the Championship. The game was an evenly fought affair until Bruce Grobbelaar committed one of the biggest blunders ever seen in a derby game. Kevin Ratcliffe shot from twenty-five yards out, but there was little pace on the ball and the Liverpool keeper looked to have it covered. Somehow the ball squirmed away from Grobbelaar and into the net.

Nobody was more surprised than Ratcliffe, and when Lineker scored his 28th goal of the season by lobbing the Liverpool keeper twelve minutes from time, Everton's day was complete. It was Lineker's one and only opportunity on goal that day, but he took it like a world-class striker.

New Everton signing Gary Lineker seen here in action against Aston Villa. Lineker was a sensational goalscorer for the Blues, scoring 38 goals in 52 appearances.

Liverpool's Alan Hansen had kept a tight rein on Lineker for practically the whole game, but the Everton goal-scoring sensation had struck with rapier precision when given the chance. What had really impressed Hansen, however, was Lineker's speed off the mark. He recalled: 'Around the mid-eighties when Liverpool and Everton were involved in some stirring encounters, there was no one quicker than Gary Lineker. I was fast, but I couldn't catch him.'

A young Evertonian who was delighted to see his heroes in blue get one over on the old enemy that winter's day was a future Liverpool star, Robbie Fowler. Fowler idolised the Everton team of the 1980s and in an interview during his Liverpool days recalled:

'I was a definite Evertonian as a lad, a dyed-in-the-wool true blue, just like my dad. My great favourites were Trevor Steven and Graeme Sharp. Trevor was an unbelievable player who could go past opponents for fun. And, in my eyes, Graeme Sharp was the complete forward – a terrific example for a young striker to follow. He would hold the ball up well, create chances and, of course, he could score goals. I remember the 1985/86 season when he partnered Gary Lineker up front for Everton and they notched up 60 goals between them.'

Everton's victory over Liverpool put them in a strong position in pursuit of their second League title in a row, but injuries to the likes of Southall, Mountfield and Reid meant that they never really looked as formidable as they had in the previous campaign. Their city rivals Liverpool refused to allow Everton to pull away from them in the League and it was only in the final few games of the season that a decisive break was made. But it was to be the Reds and not Everton who would take the spoils. A goalless draw at Manchester United followed by one of the most calamitous defeats in Everton's history, away at Oxford, cost the Blues the title. Everton followed up their 1-0 Oxford defeat with a 6-1 home victory over Southampton, but Liverpool's away victory at Chelsea gave them the League Championship. Gary Lineker notched a hat-trick against Southampton, but trouped off the pitch a dejected player after hearing that Liverpool had won at Chelsea. 'I just wish I could swap a goal today for one against Oxford last week,' he told the press.

Liverpool player-manager Kenny Dalglish was delighted with his first major success in just his first season in charge at Anfield, but he still managed a few words of praise for his Everton rivals. Dalglish said: 'Merseyside has two teams to be proud of and two who have shown their consistency by finishing first and second in the League for the past two seasons. The rest of the country must be envious. It's rivalry on Merseyside, not warfare.' Manchester United captain Bryan Robson whose team had finished a disappointing fourth after leading for more than half the season, had no doubts who he thought were the best team on Merseyside. Robson said: 'Although Liverpool won the League, I still rate Everton as the best all-round side.' Nottingham Forest manager, Brian Clough, was

Above: *An unusual shot of the entire West Ham team on the goal line attempting to defend against an Everton free-kick during the 1985/86 season.*

Right: *Pat Van den Hauwe seen here in action during the 1985/86 season. Van den Hauwe made 189 appearances for Everton before being transferred to Spurs in 1989.*

Opposite: *Neil Pointon, signed by Howard Kendall from Scunthorpe United at the end of 1985. Pointon, who cost Everton just £50,000, proved an impressive signing for the Blues, making over 100 appearances for the club during the latter half of the 1980s.*

Opposite above: *Action from the Everton v. Nottingham Forest game at Goodison Park, 1985/86 season.*

Opposite below: *Kevin Ratcliffe celebrates after scoring against Liverpool at Anfield in 1986. Despite Everton's 2-0 victory, Liverpool still went on to take the League Championship title.*

Left: *Trevor Steven, one of the classiest players ever to wear the Everton shirt. Steven appeared to glide over the pitch at times and could turn a game with one piece of football brilliance. He was a great loss to Everton when he was sold to Glasgow Rangers in 1989.*

surprised that Everton had failed to take the title. Clough remarked: 'I have long rated Everton as the best side in the country and what they have achieved over the past couple of years is nothing short of staggering. They are a young side, they have the talent, and if they can keep it together they will carry on being successful.' Although Everton would have one more season in the sun, their failure to keep the likes of Gary Lineker, Trevor Steven and Gary Stevens at the club would ultimately lead to their decline. All would leave the club prematurely, most obviously to improve their bank balance, but also in pursuit of the opportunity to play in European competitions. The aftermath of Heysel would ultimately hit Everton harder than any other English club. But first there was the small matter of stopping their greatest rivals from becoming the fifth club in history to complete the League and FA Cup double.

ten

The Clash of the Titans:
The First All-Merseyside
FA Cup Final, 1986

Howard Kendall and Kenny Dalglish lead their teams out at Wembley for the 1986 FA Cup final. Despite an opening goal from Gary Lineker, Liverpool won the trophy 3-1.

'We battered them for an hour. We had the game won. But a game is ninety minutes long, not sixty, and at the end of the day the best team wins. They held the Cup up, we didn't. I feel so sick.'

Peter Reid

Everton's 1985/86 FA Cup campaign began with a third round 1-0 win over Exeter City. Full-back Gary Stevens supplied the winner after the West Country team had provided a much sterner test than was anticipated. In the next round, two goals from Gary Lineker and one from Van den Hauwe gave the Blues a comfortable 3-1 success against Blackburn. Spurs in the fifth round provided a much tougher test at White Hart Lane. Once again it was goal king Gary Lineker who clinched victory after Adrian Heath's 50th-minute opener. Although Spurs could boast skilful players like Hoddle and Waddle, the London club adopted a strong arm approach from the start and Kevin Ratcliffe, after a brutal late tackle from Falco, had to leave the field to be replaced at centre-back by Everton's great utility man of the 1980s, Alan Harper.

Harper switched to centre-back with Richardson coming on at right-back. Still the tackles kept flying in and Roberts was booked for a lunge at Richardson. Everton continued to concentrate on their football and despite a rousing Spurs finale, during which Falco scored ten minutes from time, the Blues recorded a fine victory. After the game, Howard Kendall paid tribute to his team and to Alan Harper in particular when he said:

'They were all heroes out there. This was a win that was achieved through tremendous character. We have players who can come in, such as Alan Harper and Kevin Richardson, who when asked to do a job perform brilliantly. I would have to ask my chairman for half a million if I wanted to replace Alan Harper because I would need two good quality players to take his place.'

Everton's sixth-round opponents were Luton Town. Luton boss David Pleat, somewhat prematurely as it was to turn out, hailed Everton as the 1986 champions in his programme notes. But on the field of play, and using their much-detested (by opposition teams) artificial pitch to the maximum, Luton found themselves leading after just twenty-two minutes through a goal from Mick Harford. Graeme Sharp equalised in the second half, only for Mark Stein to restore Luton's advantage. Everton's renowned fighting spirit

came into full play as they bombarded the Luton goal and it was no surprise when Heath equalised after seventy-seven minutes. It was Everton who were pushing for the winner at the death, but the game remained at 2-2 until the end. A Gary Lineker thunderbolt gave Everton a hard-fought 1-0 victory in the replay at Goodison, with Luton pushing them close all the way. Lineker's goal came when he beat Foster and Donaghy to a long through ball from Steven and rocketed the ball past Les Sealey for an outstanding finish. Everton's victory came at a price, however, with Peter Reid limping off after just twenty minutes for treatment. Reid returned but was severely restricted in his play and would be out for several weeks for Everton as they strived to retain their title. It was left to the outstanding Paul Bracewell to virtually run Everton's central midfield single-handed as they held on for victory over Luton. Injuries had hit Everton particularly hard during the 1985/86 season with Mountfield, Southall, Reid, Van den Hauwe and Sheedy all out for long periods.

Everton's victory over Luton gave them an FA Cup semi-final against Sheffield Wednesday. Liverpool were also in the semis and would play Southampton. The first all-Merseyside FA Cup final was still a possibility. Although Evertonians were delighted to be in the running for the elusive 'double,' they were alarmed to read newspaper reports linking their manager with Spanish giants Barcelona. Terry Venables was currently in charge at the Spanish club, but a summer move to take the Goodison boss Howard Kendall to Barcelona was strongly touted. As it turned out, Kendall would remain at Goodison for one more momentous season before trying his luck abroad.

The FA Cup semi-finals coincided with Grand National Day on Merseyside, 5 April 1986 to be precise. Richard Dunwoody on board West Tip took the honours at Aintree, and it was Everton and Liverpool who fought their way through to the FA Cup final.

Opposite: *Merseyside united before the start of the 1986 FA Cup Final. Will the sight of opposing fans mixing freely, without a hint of trouble, ever be seen at a major British game again?*

Right: *Blues and Reds together, 1986.*

Liverpool beat Southampton 2-0 at White Hart Lane, and Everton defeated Sheffield Wednesday 2-1 at Villa Park. Graeme Sharp was Everton's hero when he scored the winner in extra-time. Everton lined up for the game without the injured trio of Southall, Sheedy and Lineker, and Trevor Steven also had to leave the field after just thirty minutes with a groin strain. Against a strong Wednesday team, who went on to finish fifth in the First Division, injury-hit Everton knew it would be hard to reach the final. It was Everton who took the lead through Alan Harper, but Shutt equalised for the Sheffield team just sixty seconds later. Ninety minutes play failed to find a winner and it was in injury time that Everton came out on top. Once again, Paul Bracewell was having an outstanding game, and it was Bracewell who set up the winning goal when he sent a ball through the Sheffield defence to Sharp, who with Sterland climbing all over him still managed to retain his composure and direct a shot high into the roof of the net. Everton's trademark inner-strength enabled them to ward off anything Sheffield Wednesday threw at them for the remainder of extra-time and they were through to Wembley for their third FA Cup final in succession.

Howard Kendall and his Everton team were ecstatic. Despite their crippling injury list they had still managed to win through. Graeme Sharp was universally praised by the football media for his performance and Kendall joined in the tributes to the Scot when he said: 'Graeme was tremendous. He fully deserved his winner and you'll have to go a long way to see a better exhibition of forward play.' Everton's stand-in goalkeeper, Bobby Mimms, also had a tremendous game and Kendall praised the young keeper: 'If we can turn round at the end of the season and say that we have not missed Neville Southall, it will be a tremendous compliment to Bobby Mimms. He has played three big games for us in a week and I can honestly say that.'

Gary Lineker in action against Liverpool during the FA Cup final, 1986.

The semi–final success of the two Merseyside giants sent the city into a frenzy as the search for Cup final tickets hotted up. Only 50,000 tickets were allocated to the two sets of supporters, with an estimated six times that number wanting to attend the Wembley final. Gary Lineker, who missed the semi–final, had another double celebration that triumphant weekend when he was selected as the PFA 'Player of the Year' and also the football writers' 'Footballer of the Year.' Gary Lineker had scored 36 club and international goals already, and former England great Bobby Charlton said of Lineker:

> 'His record this year speaks volumes for his knack in front of goal. He's so fast off the mark that he makes chances out of nothing. He has great vision and that uncanny knack of being in the right place at the right time. When it comes to the business of finishing accurately, he is lethal. He has developed from being a superb player at Leicester to a great player at Everton.'

With the FA Cup final against Liverpool on the agenda, the magic goal-scoring boots of Gary Lineker would have to be at their best if Everton were going to succeed at Wembley.

Everton's failure to hold on to their League title by the narrowest of margins to Liverpool made them doubly determined to prevent the Reds clinching the double, and the debate raged before the game as to who would come out on top, with both teams appearing to be so evenly matched. Luton boss David Pleat told the press: 'Everton have got tremendous resilience and team spirit, plus terrific determination to make up for the ten years of lost time with Liverpool.' Graham Taylor also backed Everton and he said: 'Everton are now as good a side as Liverpool. They can now give Liverpool a game anywhere at any time.' Bobby Robson found it hard to split the two teams: 'How do you choose? There is so little between them. The difference is paper-thin. Ian Rush and Kenny Dalglish for Liverpool, Gary Lineker and Graeme Sharp for Everton.' Liverpool's legendary former manager, Bob Paisley, praised the Everton team that Howard Kendall had assembled and let it slip that Liverpool had also tried to sign Gary Lineker before Everton landed him. He said:

'Everton haven't paid huge prices for players, then turned them onto the pitch and asked for special individual skills. Everton are not necessarily the best individuals in the League, but they have become very, very good when moulded together. Peter Reid has been a major influence and Gary Lineker has scored a lot of goals this season. It is true that we were after him, but we don't cry over spilt milk. Lineker may not have suited Liverpool as he has suited Everton.'

Everton's midfield star Paul Bracewell was hoping to use the final to stake a final claim for a place in England's 1986 World Cup party. He had been outstanding during the periods in the season when his midfield partner, Peter Reid, had been out injured. Bracewell compared the Merseyside derby to those that he had played in the North East during his Sunderland days, and said: 'I've played in Sunderland v. Newcastle derbies but they are very different affairs to Merseyside ones, mainly because there is more hostility between the supporters. Unlike in Liverpool, you can't imagine Sunderland and Newcastle fans going to the match together.'

On the morning of the game, television coverage centred on the two strikers Ian Rush and Gary Lineker. Who would come out on top, Wales or England? Most of the football pundits found it impossible to separate the two. Former goalscoring great, Jimmy Greaves, couldn't divide Rush or Lineker either. Greaves said:

'At Wembley today we will see two of the best strikers of the last twenty-five years. You can mention them in the same breath as George Best and Denis Law. My only regret is that Rushie was born the wrong side of the Welsh border. I can't choose between Gary and Ian. I've been a Lineker fan from the first time I saw him play for Leicester. I kept nagging Ron Atkinson to buy him for Manchester United, but he ignored me.'

Kevin Ratcliffe was determined not to give his international team-mate Ian Rush any chances during the game. Rush had made a habit of putting Everton to the sword over recent years but this time, Ratcliffe said, it would be different. He said: 'Ian Rush is a good mate of mine. We live in north Wales and when he was banned from driving I used to give him a lift to training. He certainly won't be getting any favours at Wembley in the final.'

Despite Ratcliffe's determination to stop the Welsh goal-scoring machine, it was Ian Rush who would ultimately break Evertonians' hearts with two goals at Wembley that afternoon on 10 May 1986. Everton had started the game brightly, and it was no surprise when Lineker latched on to a thirty-yard pass from Reid and outsprinted the Liverpool defence to score. Everton were in control of the game until the second-half, when Liverpool suddenly clicked into gear and Rush equalised. Just six minutes later Craig Johnston put Liverpool into the lead when he scored from a Molby cross. Everton pressed hard for an equaliser, but their fate was sealed when Rush shot past the hapless Bobby Mimms to give Liverpool the cup. Liverpool had completed the League and FA Cup double for the first time in their history. But it could so easily have been Everton. A season that had promised so much had turned sour at the final hurdles in both the League and the Cup. Barcelona manager Terry Venables was at Wembley to check on the form of Gary Lineker. Venables would within weeks persuade the Barcelona board to bid close to £3 million for the lethal striker. Howard Kendall obviously did not want to lose Lineker, but refused to stand in his way. Everton had not just lost the double by a whisker, but also one of the greatest strikers that British football had seen. If Everton had been allowed to play in Europe it is unlikely that Lineker would have been quite so tempted to quit Goodison. But the lure of Barcelona and pitting his skills against the best in Europe proved too much of a temptation. The curse of Heysel had hit Everton again and it would ultimately cost them their manager.

Everton and Liverpool share the Charity Shield after a 1-1 draw at Wembley.

eleven

Howard Kendall's
Swansong: Champions
Again, 1987

Kevin Ratcliffe in action against Liverpool during Everton's title-winning 1986/87 season.

'Howard Kendall's great strengths are that he is a thinker, intense and ambitious. Part of the Everton success story has been his combination with Colin Harvey.'

Alan Ball

As expected, Everton began the 1986/87 season without Gary Lineker. His sensational exploits in the World Cup, when he finished the tournament as leading scorer with six goals, prompted Barcelona to agree to Everton's asking price. All of this was little consolation to Evertonians. Although Lineker was originally not universally acclaimed by all at Goodison, the majority soon realised that the England striker was a special talent. But the Lineker season had been trophy-less and there would be another major honour to savour before Everton's glory days of the 1980s would come to an end. Everton's two pre-season signings, Paul Power for just £65,000 from Manchester City, and Dave Watson for a club record £900,000 from Norwich City, would become key members of Everton's Championship-winning side. The signing of thirty-two-year-old Mancunian Power surprised many at Goodison, but once again Kendall was to prove how astute he was in the transfer market. Dave Watson took some time to win over the doubters at Everton. Watson had replaced the popular Derek Mountfield in the centre of defence. Mountfield had suffered badly from injury the previous season, but the Goodison regulars were keen to see him back in the team once match-fit. Although Mountfield did recover from his torn cartilage, and replaced Watson in the Everton line-up for a brief period during the 1986/87 season, it would be Dave Watson who was to finally make the place his own. The fact that Watson would go on to make 476 appearances for the Blues is testimony to the fact that Everton's record signing of 1986 was destined to become a future Goodison legend.

Paul Power, after eleven seasons at Manchester City, during which he had hardly won a thing, could not believe his good fortune when told that Howard Kendall wanted him to join a Championship-chasing club at Everton. The superbly fit Power filled in for the injured Pat Van den Hauwe on the left side of defence, and also for Kevin Sheedy in midfield when the demand arose. His performance level was so high during the 1986/87 season that Power tied with Kevin Ratcliffe for the Everton supporters' 'Player of the Year' trophy.

With Gary Lineker no longer in the team, the goals for Everton now came from all sections of the team. Despite the fact that Everton began the season with Bracewell, Reid, Van den Hauwe, Southall and Mountfield all out injured, the team remained

Left: *Ian Snodin arrives at Goodison with his brother Glyn after signing for Everton in January 1987. Liverpool were also keen to sign the Leeds midfielder, but Everton were his choice. Snodin went on to become a crucial member of the 1987 title-winning team. He cost Everton £840,000.*

Below: *Ian Snodin enjoys a cup of tea after signing for the Blues in 1987.*

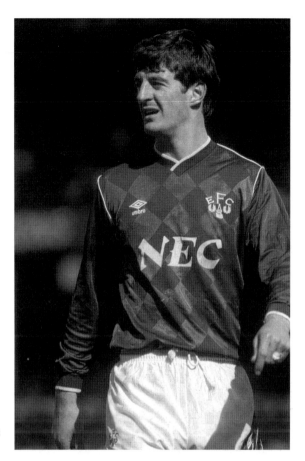

Wayne Clarke signed for Everton in March 1987 and scored vital goals in their pursuit of the League Championship. Clarke cost Everton £300,000 from Birmingham City.

unbeaten in the opening seven games. Alan Harper was once again proving his fantastic versatility, filling-in a number of roles and playing 29 times during the Championship-winning campaign. With Everton's ongoing injury list in mind, Howard Kendall signed the outstanding Leeds' midfielder Ian Snodin for £840,000 in January 1987. Liverpool had also been in the hunt for Snodin, but his choice was Everton and he became a key member of the title-winning team. Another piece of astute transfer business from Kendall brought Wayne Clarke to Goodison for a £300,000 fee from Birmingham. Although not really of the same calibre as his older brother Allan, Wayne Clarke certainly knew how to put the ball into the net and would be crucial in Everton's run-in to the title.

As the season unfolded, the title chase was like a game of pass-the-parcel with Spurs, Wimbledon, Nottingham Forest, Arsenal and then Liverpool all taking turns at the top. Liverpool took over the leadership with a run of 10 victories in 12 games, but Everton gradually began to make up ground on the Reds. Showing remarkable consistency, they lost just four of their final 29 League games. Everton clinched the title at Norwich when Pat Van den Hauwe hit a sensational opening goal after just forty-five seconds of play. Everton retained their lead to give Howard Kendall his second League Championship as manager. A few days later at Goodison Park it was party time as the trophy was presented to Kevin Ratcliffe before they trounced Luton 3-1, the goals coming from Trevor Steven, with two, and Graeme Sharp. As the delirious Evertonians chanted,

Kevin Ratcliffe – he captained Everton to another League Championship in 1987.

Paul Bracewell, an outstanding Everton midfielder during the double-winning 1984/85 season. Bracewell was on the verge of becoming an England regular when an injury sustained at Newcastle on New Year's Day 1986 brought his career to a sudden halt. Bracewell did return to the Everton team following several operations on a piece of loose bone that caused severe pain in his ankle, but Evertonians were never to witness again the form that the dynamic Bracewell displayed before his injury problems. Along with Lineker, Steven, and Stevens, another great talent was lost to Everton as the great mid-1980s team began to disband. Bracewell rejoined Sunderland in 1989 but he was not the same player.

'Champions, Champions', little did they know that the man who had led the club to two League titles, the European Cup Winners' Cup and the FA Cup, all within six years, would soon be leaving to try his luck in Europe with Spanish club Atletic Bilbao.

Howard Kendall's departure stunned Evertonians. There had been reports the previous season that Barcelona were lining him up to replace Terry Venables, but they had decided to keep their cockney manager and take Gary Lineker from Everton instead. The majority of Blues fans were delighted to hear that the highly-respected Colin Harvey was to be appointed the new Everton manager. The Everton board had approached Harvey the previous year when they too suspected that Kendall might leave for Barcelona, but their fears proved to be unfounded. Colin Harvey had proved himself to be an outstanding coach during Everton's trophy-winning period, but as a manager he failed to bring any more honours to Goodison. Losing international-class players such as Gary Stevens to Rangers in 1989 and Trevor Steven, who had top-scored for Everton with fourteen goals during their 1986/87 title-winning season, also to Rangers in 1989, did not help him. But both of them, like Kendall, were keen to face a new challenge playing against European opposition. They were not going to achieve that ambition at Goodison Park.

Left: *Gary Stevens. The England international was a great servant to Everton during the glory days of the mid-1980s.*

Opposite above: *Kevin Ratcliffe displays the First Division Championship trophy after Everton's victorious 1986/87 campaign.*

Opposite below: *The Everton championship-winning team of 1986/87.*

The unassuming Harvey would probably have admitted himself that managing Everton did not really suit his personality; bringing new talent on and putting his players through their paces on the training ground, rather than facing the media, being more his forte. Colin Harvey's three-year record as Everton manager would have probably kept him in a managerial position for life at some clubs – FA Cup finalists, League Cup semi-finals, fourth, eighth and sixth in the League – but Evertonians had had a golden period of success and were eager to taste some more. Sadly, when Howard Kendall returned to the club in 1990 with Colin Harvey as his assistant, the glory days of the 1980s were fast becoming a fading memory, but hopefully one day they will return.

*Kevin Ratcliffe, being interviewed by Charles Lambert at BBC Radio Merseyside after Everton's 1987
Championship success.*

Above: *Everton parade the Charity Shield around Wembley after their 1987 victory over Coventry.*

Left: *Colin Harvey takes over as Everton manager at the start of the 1987/88 season. Howard Kendall decided to try his luck at Athletic Bilbao but returned to Goodison at the end of 1990.*

Howard Kendall returned to Everton in November 1990 with Colin Harvey as his assistant. The glory days of the 1980s, however, were by now a fading memory.

Bibliography

Steve McMahon with Harry Harris, *Macca Can! The Steve McMahon Story*, Pelham Books, 1990.

Kevin Ratcliffe, *The Blues and I,* Arthur Barker, 1988.

Ian Ross & Gordon Smailes, *Everton A Complete Record 1878-1985*, Breedon Books, 1985.

Howard Kendall, *Howard Kendall's Everton Scrapbook*, Souvenir Press, 1986.

Gary Stevens & Trevor Steven, with Dave Smith, *Even Stevens*, Mainstream Publishing, 1988.

Ivan Ponting, *Everton Player by Player*, Hamlyn, 1998.

Andy Gray, *Shades Of Gray*, Macdonald Queen Anne Press, 1986.

Ric George, *Everton Football Club*, (*Liverpool Echo*) Archive Publications Ltd, 1989.

Andrew Longmore, *Viv Anderson*, Heinemann, 1988.

Jon Berman and Malcolm Dome, *Everton Greats – Where Are They Now?*, Mainstream Publishing, 1997.

Roger Taylor and AndrewWard, with John Williams *Three Sides of The Mersey – An oral history of Everton, Liverpool and Tranmere Rovers*, Robson Books, 1993.

Andy Gray with Jim Drewitt, *Flat Back Four - The Tactical Game,* Boxtree, 1999.

Dennis Signy and Norman Giller, *Golden Heroes: Fifty Seasons of Footballer of the Year,* Chameleon Books, 1997.

Michael Heatley and Ian Welch, *Liverpool versus Everton, A complete history of the fixture,* Dial House, 1996.

Brian Barwick and Gerald Sinstadt, *Everton v. Liverpool: A celebration of the Merseyside Derby,* BBC Books, 1988.

Peter Reid with Peter Ball, *Everton Winter Mexican Summer: A Football Diary,* Queen Anne Press, 1987.

The Liverpool Echo

The Liverpool Daily Post

The Liverpool Football Echo

The Mirror

The Star

The Daily Express

The Guardian

The Times

The Daily Telegraph

The Sunday Mirror

Special thanks: Mrs Phil Jackson; James Howarth and all at Tempus Publishing.